ACKNOWLEDGEMENTS

I am indebted to those who have given their permission to include extracts from early press articles about my late father, including: *The Fife Free Press, The Courier & Advertiser, The Illustrated London News,* and *The People's Journal.*

My grateful thanks also go to The Orion Publishing Group, publishers of *Winged Dagger* (1948) by Roy Farran, though attempts to trace the copyright holder of this book were unsuccessful and to Collins, publishers of *The Black Watch and the King's Enemies* (1950) by Bernard Fergusson.

I very much appreciate the support and encouragement given by Major Ronnie Proctor, MBE, FSA Scotland, Secretary of The Black Watch Association. Fiona Connah, Museum Assistant at Balhousie Castle, Regimental Museum of The Black Watch, needs thanking for her help in providing access to the museum's holdings relating to Pipe Major Robert Roy.

Pipe Major Alistair Duthie, Steve Zajda, Jean Hands, Ronnie Proctor, Stuart McAdam, and Sir Alistair Irwin all read through drafts of this book making helpful comments. All this effort is greatly appreciated. Any mistakes that remain however are my own.

Lastly, thanks go to Roben Antoniewicz, Bernard Chandler, Zack Fummey, Rob Hands, Matthew Mackie, and Paul Philippou for the editorial work, photographs, maps, book design, and cover.

'Recommended for the award of the Victoria Cross for exceptional and continuous gallantry. The playing of his pipes, without doubt, encouraged the battalion, despite the heavy casualties they were incurring from enemy machine gun fire, which there was insufficient artillery to neutralise, to achieve its object.'

'On 21 November 1941 Pipe Major Roy displayed the most exceptional and outstanding gallantry and devotion to duty in the attack of the battalion on 'Tiger' from the Tobruk Perimeter.

From the start line to the German battalion position commanding the objective, he played his pipes with the foremost troops almost continuously throughout the advance of 2½ miles, under heavy enemy fire of all kinds for the entire distance.

When collective movement ceased, and while the enemy position was being reduced, the Pipe Major crawled round to the wounded men near him, dressing wounds and giving them water, when any movement brought down a hail of enemy fire.

In the vicinity of the objective he was ordered back to the R.A.P. having been wounded three times.

His bravery and example of complete disregard of personal danger was an inspiration to the advancing troops and had a direct bearing on maintaining the impetus of the attack.

This N.C.O. previously distinguished himself in the defence of Crete where he was again wounded and captured by the enemy. On recovery, he escaped from a P.O.W. camp in Greece and at considerable personal danger made his way back to Syria where he rejoined the battalion.'

Unit: 2nd Black Watch.
Regimental Number: 2216492.
Recommendations: Lieutenant-Colonel G. A.
Rusk, MC – Commander 2nd Black Watch.
Eye Witness Notifications: Captain N. Boyle,
Captain J. Ewan, RSM R. G. Young.

'Recommended for the MBE in Respect of Queen's Birthday 1956 by Lieutenant-Colonel W. J. Campbell Adamson, TD, OC 4/5th Battalion, The Black Watch (TA).'

'RSM Roy is an excellent RSM to this battalion. He carries out all of his duties with zeal and enthusiasm far above the ordinary and spares neither his own time, nor his personal convenience in order to further the efficiency and well-being of the unit.

In addition to this, and quite apart from his regular duty, he has given a very great deal of his time, and much effort, to the cadets of the affiliated Cadet Battalion. His enthusiasm and help have resulted in the 1st Dundee Cadet Battalion's Pipes and Drums. This, in its turn, has helped the Cadet Battalion to attract boys and give them a pride in their unit, and has produced the more far-reaching result of attracting regular recruits to the Army.

It is no exaggeration to say that by his efforts, and through his reputation, RSM Roy has become a public figure in this part of Scotland, and that his every action rebounds to the general credit of the Army far beyond the normal capacity of a man of his rank.'

Place: Dundee and Angus.
Period Covered: 9 May 1952 – 10 January 1956.
How Employed: RSM in 4/5th Battalion,
The Black Watch (TA).

CONTENTS

LIST OF ILLUSTRATIONS AND PHOTOGRAPHS

*All photographs in Photograph Sections 1 and 2 are
taken from the 'Author's Collection' unless otherwise stated.
All maps by Rob Hands.
All photographs in Photograph Section 3 are
by Roben Antoniewicz.*

PHOTOGRAPH SECTION 1
(after Chapter 2)
'Beginnings, Palestine, Crete, Greece, and Syria'

1. Agnes Roy (*née* Riddell).

2. No. 2 Section, F Company, the 2nd Battalion, The Black Watch, India, 1898. William Roy, second row, third from left.

3. All India Hockey Tournament Allahabad, India, 1900, Winner: The Black Watch.

4. Robert Roy, The Black Watch, centre.

5. Rutherglen Pipe Band, Largs War Memorial. Robert Roy, sixth from right.

6. Presentation of new Colours to the 2nd Battalion, The Black Watch, Balmoral Castle, 14th September 1937. Robert Roy – on far left.

7. Christmas/New Year card from Jerusalem, Palestine, 1937 or 1938.

8. Pipe Band, Jerusalem, Palestine.

9. In Palestine or India. Robert Roy on right.

10. Decorative brass plate commemorating the service of the 2nd Battalion, The Black Watch, Palestine, 1937-9, formerly belonging to Corporal W. S. Latto of the Battalion's Signals Section. Black Watch Museum (A5739 – on display). *Photograph: Roben Antoniewicz.*

PHOTOGRAPH SECTION 2
(after Chapter 9)
'Tobruk, Germany, Scotland, and Gibraltar'

29. Trafalgar Square on day of Robert Roy's MBE award at Buckingham Palace, 31st May 1956. Left to right: Margaret, Hilda, and Alice.

30. Marriage of Brigadier Bernard Fergusson to Laura Margaret Grenfell, 22nd November 1950.

31. Robert Roy as Gibraltar Garrison Sergeant Major.

32. Left to right: Lance Corporal J. Grieve, General Eisenhower, and Pipe Major Robert Roy.

33. 5th Group Gibraltar Sea Scouts Band, 14th June 1960.

PHOTOGRAPH SECTION 3
(after Chapter 10)
'Pipe Major Robert Roy – Balhousie Castle, Regimental Museum of The Black Watch, Perth – Holdings'

34. Balhousie Castle, Regimental Museum of The Black Watch, Perth.

35. Blue bonnet hackle belonging to Regimental Sergeant Major Robert Roy. (2012.94.9 – in store)

36. Brown leather piper's cross belt belonging to Pipe Major Robert Roy. (2012.94.4 – in store)

37. Green Jacket, 'No. 1 Dress', with three rows of Medal Ribbons plus 'Mention in Dispatches', eighteen buttons, 'Warrant Officer Class 1' badge on sleeve belonging to Regimental Sergeant Major Robert Roy. (A2698 – in store)

38. Green khaki jacket, with full length sleeves with turned up cuffs and Lion Decoration on sleeve, shoulder straps fastened with silver Black Watch buttons, left and right waist and breast pockets with flap, fastened with four buttons, ribbons above left breast pocket [enlargement inset]: War Defence Medal; British Empire, Imperial Service Order; General Service Medal 1918-62, 1939-45 Star, Africa Star; Burma Star, France Germany Star, Defence Medal, Second World War Medal with Oak Leaf pin; Army LS & GC Second Type, Second World War Service Medal, belonging to Regimental Sergeant Major Robert Roy. (2012.94.2 – in store)

FOREWORD

AS A YOUNG BOY growing up in Kirriemuir, Angus, in the 1950s and as a member of the Army Cadet Force, Rab Roy 'the Piper of Tobruk' became one of my heroes after I had read of his exploits in one of the comic books which were popular at that time. He remained so throughout my 40 years' service as a junior then adult member of The Black Watch and remains so to the present day.

As a young soldier I listened in awe as those who had served with him told of his exploits, from his escape from the Germans in Greece after being captured in Crete and reporting back to his Battalion in Syria, to his heroism and bravery at Tobruk where he played the Second Battalion, The Black Watch, into battle. Despite being wounded he continued to play his pipes and also tend the wounded.

Later as Curator of the Black Watch Museum nothing gave me greater pleasure than to show visitors of all nationalities his bullet riddled Royal Stewart piper's kilt and the photographs of him having his wounds tended to which were on display along with other artefacts.

Visiting Crete and assisting on battlefield tours to educate young Black Watch soldiers gave me great pleasure to walk in the footsteps of this gallant and heroic man.

His daughter Alice has done her father proud by painstakingly drawing together all the facts regarding her heroic but humble father's life and has confirmed that Pipe Major Rab Roy, MBE, DCM, 'The Piper of Tobruk' was a true hero both in war and in peace and is truly worthy of a place in our nation's history.

RONNIE PROCTOR, MBE, FSA SCOTLAND
Secretary of The Black Watch Association

PREFACE

'**THE PIPER OF TOBRUK**' is about my late father, Pipe Major Robert Roy, MBE, DCM, of The Black Watch who became known as 'The Piper of Tobruk'. Not only does it describe his heroic action at Tobruk, one of the fiercest battles of the Second World War, as well as his extensive military career in India, Greece, Germany, and Britain, but also the difficult personal issues he faced when he fell in love with my German mother at the end of that war.

The book contains my father's own written accounts of his involvement in battle and capture in Crete, his escape from Athens, copies of forged identity documents he used to travel through Turkey and Syria to re-join his Regiment in North Africa, and letters from Greek allies and friends that highlight my father's friendship and their respect for him. Having astounded his commanding officer by walking into the camp in civilian disguise, my father then went on to display outstanding bravery at Tobruk, supported by a range of evidence from old newspapers and accounts from writers such as Sir Bernard Fergusson (The Black Watch) and Roy Farran (SAS), and the citations for his DCM and MBE awards.

Although finally spending well-earned time in Britain after Tobruk, my father then volunteered for action in Europe, leading to the Rhine crossing and Allied control in Germany where, in 1946 in Duisburg, he met my mother. His personal correspondence, which I have included, highlights the unsuccessful attempts made to discredit him because of his association with the 'enemy' and illustrate perhaps the most difficult challenge of all for this brave man.

Post-war years are also described, showing my father's continuing career in the Territorial Army, with photographs of him at various events such as meeting the Queen Mother with General Wavell, with General Eisenhower at SHAPE (Supreme Headquarters Allied Powers Europe), as well as congratulatory letters on his MBE.

Meantime, on the domestic front, my father twice tried unsuccessfully to find council housing in his home city of Glasgow, proving nothing has changed since 1948!

Finding an old suitcase full of documents, letters, photographs, and newspaper cuttings led to my writing this book, which contains not only previously unseen information but also provided the opportunity to piece together and tell the story of the life of a very brave, interesting yet humble man who served his country well.

Alice Soper
Spring 2019

CHAPTER 1

BEGINNINGS

ROBERT ROY was born in June 1909 in Glasgow, where the Roy family had moved from Perthshire, home of The Black Watch (Royal Highland Regiment), in the late 1800s. His father, also named Robert, and his brothers William and James had served in the Regiment, spending tours of duty in India and South Africa in the late 1890s.

On leaving the army, my grandfather and his brother William had married sisters Agnes and Mary Riddell and had settled in the Camlachie district of Glasgow, working for Alex Hodge, carter contractor. Encouraged by my grandfather, my father learned to play the bagpipes and by the age of thirteen, when he was employed as a 'trace boy', he practised at Beardman's Hall (the Forge). By fourteen, he was a 'skilly' piper member of Stewart's & Lloyds' (Rutherglen) Pipe Band.

It was no surprise that Robert Roy too opted for a military career, enlisting at Rutherglen in the Royal Engineers (Territorial Army), in the 52nd (Lowland) Division, at the age of sixteen. Robert Roy subsequently enlisted in The Black Watch 23rd November 1926 when he was seventeen, though his age was stated as being eighteen. He served in Britain between 1926 and December 1929, followed by fourteen months in India, reaching the end of his first enlistment on 2nd March 1931. After 19 months as a civilian, he re-enlisted 24th October 1932 (at Perth) – transferring to Section A, Army Reserve, King's Regulations.

During this time, personal tragedy struck with three family bereavements. Firstly, the death of his 95-year-old great grandmother Agnes (Rollo) Wedderspoon, on 14th February 1926 in Edinburgh. Then the following November, her daughter, my father's grandmother Jane Roy, aged 77 years, in Glasgow. She had suffered a cerebral

THE PIPER OF TOBRUK

haemorrhage twelve days previously. My grandfather, who by this
time had worked for many years as a carter for Alex Hodge, was
proud of his son's achievements and looked forward to his leave
visits, but further tragedy was soon to come.

Some time before December 1929, my grandfather became ill
and a few weeks later, just as my father was posted to India, he
underwent an operation. He never fully recovered and tragically
died, aged 54, on 30th January 1931 in Glasgow Cancer Hospital.
The family was supported by its wider family and friends, and in
July that year, a cousin wrote to my father thanking him for Indian
shawls he had sent, saying:

> **Received shawls. Taking one to the nurse and one to
> Alex Hodge's wife as they have been that good to us
> the whole time your father was in hospital.**

My father's army career progressed well. In 1932, he was again
fully enlisted with The Black Watch and was now a proficient piper.
From these early years onwards, he won several silver cups for
piping, including a first in the 1935 'Buddon Regimental Piobaireachd'.
He would go on to compose several bagpipe tunes over the years
including *Sarafand*, written while he was in Syria in 1937. The
Black Watch published this tune many years later, in 2008, in its
collection of pipe music played in the Regiment.

Further family sadness occurred when on 28th June 1935, my
father's 61-year-old uncle William died of heart failure at home in
Bluevale Street, Glasgow, leaving his wife Mary a widow like her
sister. At that time, William's son, also called Robert Roy, a drum
major with The Black Watch, was on active service in India, so, in his
place, my father led the hearse and funeral procession on its long
journey from Bluevale Street to Riddrie Park Cemetery, playing his
bagpipes as he walked along the entire route.

That same year, the commanding officer of The Black Watch,
Lieutenant Colonel Chalmers, DSO, MC, issued orders at Barry
Buddon Camp for my father to attend a course of instruction for

army pipers to be held in Edinburgh between September 1935 and February 1936. My father was then promoted to Lance Corporal, replacing a Lance Corporal Summers.

No-one expected the shock that followed on 28th December 1936 when my father was home on leave. His mother Agnes, who had recently moved to a new home in London Road, Glasgow, set off that evening to visit the missionary John Marshall and his wife, but was fatally injured by a vehicle in the street near her home. Robert's younger brothers and sisters, Neil, David, Jessie, and Mary were then aged between ten and sixteen.

CHAPTER 2

PALESTINE TO GREECE

IN 1937, my father was promoted to the rank of sergeant, appointed Pipe Major of the 2nd Battalion, The Black Watch and was in active service in the Palestinian revolt (the 'Great Revolt') against British imperial rule and the huge influx of Jewish immigrants when war was declared in September 1939. His battalion immediately switched to the Suez Canal Zone and from there to Somaliland, where after the Italian conquest of British Somaliland, they were eventually evacuated by the Royal Navy and sent to Cairo. During this time, a young piper, Bill Lark, joined the pipe band.

There was speculation about action in the Western Desert (the desert areas of Egypt and Libya), though for a short time the units in Cairo enjoyed some deserved leisure time. By November 1940, the 2nd Battalion had been warned to stand by to move to a new, as yet unknown, destination. It was only after a 20-hour voyage and an attack by three Italian torpedo bombers that the men found themselves arriving at Suda Bay in Crete.

Meanwhile, my father's younger brother Neil had enlisted in The Black Watch on 25th March 1938, serving also in Palestine between 1938 and 1939. He spent the next two years in the UK with the Highland Regiment, 10th Battalion & 8ITC, and was delighted to let his brother know he had become a full corporal. He wrote to my father saying, 'got on alright on my course with Ross. He was asking for you'.

Although at first, life in Crete was relatively peaceful, air raids increased and the news from Greece became worse. On 16th May 1941, enemy planes attacked and by 20th May parachutists were tumbling out of the sky. Although many paratroopers were killed as they landed, the dropping continued and the German soldiers who landed safely lost no time in finding suitable cover. My father lost comrades during the battle, including Sergeants Jim Hindmarsh and Chris Wilkin, whose photographs he kept in a memorial scrapbook.

After a week of fighting, the Germans gradually worked out where to drop fresh troops and focused on the hospital site at Villa Ariadne, where there were no British soldiers to spare for its protection. The Villa Ariadne, originally built by archaeologist Sir Arthur Evans when he was excavating the palace of King Minos two hundred yards away, had been treated as neutral ground, helping both British and German wounded.

Eventually almost all the injured British troops, including my father who had been wounded twice – firstly on 21st May 1941 (right chest) and then again five days later (right shoulder) – were captured. The main British force was then told on the 28th that it would be evacuated from the island that night.

My father described his experience in two letters to Bernard Fergusson, his commanding officer who subsequently wrote *The Black Watch and the King's Enemies* (Collins, 1950) and later became Governor General of New Zealand. Fergusson had known my father since 1931, at the very beginning of his own service, when every platoon had its own piper. My father was then 23 and was described by Fergusson as, 'already the mixture of stolidity and romance that became such a familiar figure later on'.

Fergusson added:

> He was already a good piper and player of 'Piobaireachd', with a large repertoire, and was inexhaustible on the longest of marches. He had in his possession a platoon photograph of those days, showing him standing solemnly at the end of the back row, with his pipes.

In my father's first account, he described the arrival in Crete and subsequent events.

It all started so suddenly that at times I thought it was a bad dream, yet sometimes I look back with longing for those adventurous days of the past which are marred by one thing – the valiant comrades who fell in battle and those who did not make the break from the prison camp and who have languished for nearly four years now in Germany.

The beginning of May 1941 found my battalion part of the garrison of the island of Crete, having been approximately one month on the island. Our arrival on the island was greeted with quiet reserve, but as is usual with the Scottish soldier we soon broke down the reserve of this proud island race who really had so much in common with us Scottish and looked with trusting eyes on us as representatives of the strong power of Britain, who could not go under – and we were equally confident.

Our brigade was all regular army and was of a high standard, which was later proved beyond doubt and on Greece falling, we took the field in real earnest awaiting invasion either by sea or air; in full confidence that the great British Navy would attend to the sea threat and we would deal with a paratroop landing on our part of the island, which was the Chania area, with the aerodrome of Heraklion as our battalion's job to keep from being invaded.

So far, except for an occasional raid, life was very peaceful and could be described as what one soldier on this island said: "We are all living in Paradise". But this was a fool's paradise which the 21st of May awoke to, as the forenoon started with an air bombardment with short bursts but increasing in power and machine gun fire towards the late afternoon. Towards 5 pm I was given a message to take up my battle position with my men at a corner in the village and on reaching our position, we all viewed for the first time a paratroop landing which seemed to chill one watching the small white circles getting larger and larger until the men were clearly seen.

The Germans hitting the ground brought us back to the business of war and our sector was speedily cleared and as we appeared to be getting stragglers from the town on our right and the aerodrome on our left, we had no very hard job except for odd Huns who had evaded us and were sniping at us from houses.

One and a half hours fighting was all I was destined to see as about 6.30 pm I was standing in my trench to view a house that was thought to have a sniper when I suddenly felt a force like a hammer hit me on the chest, which half turned me round before I dropped with my first wound in the war. I was not heartened when an officer on coming to relieve me asked my men if the pipe major was dead yet.

On assuring him I was still very much alive I was assisted to the Regimental Aid Post [RAP] of the 7th Medium Regiment. After three days in the RAP I found myself in the field hospital at Knossos occupying a corner of a tent. This hospital by this time was catering for British and German casualties, it being by this time in a sort of neutral land, and here my contact with the Germans began. At this time there were more German wounded in this hospital. In fairness to the enemy, it was plain that he had declared a sort of neutral zone around the hospital and British or German personnel coming to the hospital on duty had to leave their arms at the gate. This resulted in both sides rubbing shoulders but, strange as it may seem, no unpleasantness occurred.

As I had to stand at the gate and do a turn of duty at seeing British disarmed before coming in, I was in a position to see that the Hun was getting in a bad way, in particular in relation to water. A large percentage in a worn-out condition was visiting the hospital for no other reason than to get water. It must also be understood that although the German troops were in bigger numbers than ours, he was supplying no food to the hospital. As we knew he could not be short of supplies we could only conclude that he was not being able to collect his supplies in full after being dropped by the air. This was borne out when news came that some of our men had found that by firing a white light very little food was dropped, which must have caused considerable annoyance. It was also noticed that if Swastika flags were laid out in a sort of square his aircraft would not bomb or machine gun that area.

The type of man in this paratroop division we were fighting appeared to be good and as far as I could see were mainly Austrians, and we all lined up for food in one go and as is nearly always found in front line troops nothing other than a correct attitude was shown by us towards the Germans who were our prisoners at this time. The same can be said about them when we became their prisoners, which was in contrast to our later experiences.

We had heard that Malame Aerodrome had fallen, and that part of the island captured. The troops at that end were having it hard and had lost a lot of ground. It had drifted back that the Welsh regiment who had relieved us at Galatas had been through hell and lost heavily. The bulk of the army at this time consisted of Australians and New Zealanders who had been through the previous campaign on the Greek mainland and later evacuated to Crete, worn out and battle weary and ill. But we were not prepared for the news which a German (and a very surprised one at that) imparted to us on 1st June at about 10 am which was that the British had evacuated in the night. I learnt later that our brigade had been ordered to evacuate and that in the ten days' fighting had still regained their ground in spite of the fact they had no aircraft support. With sinking hearts, we realised that we were now wounded prisoners.

After about a week, we were all moved to the aerodrome and handed over to a different regiment who must have come over after the island had fallen. We now experienced a different type of German who did not seem to think prisoners required food and we would lay for nearly days [sic] without any till a paratroop officer came along and got us some biscuits and chocolate.

The business of transporting us to Greece now began and the irony of fate is strange. Six months before, we had practised emplaning using forms, but never had one real try out on a plane and when we had been marched to our various transports and embarked fourteen men to a plane, I feel sure they must all have felt as I did, which was after all our training our first real trip should be in a German plane under German control.

Again, being under the fighting soldiers everything was quite pleasant and after a journey of about one and a half hours we landed outside Athens and after a wait of about a couple of hours were put on lorries. I noted again we were under base 'wallahs' who acted true to style and noted that stretcher cases got no consideration and were loaded on the three-ton lorries. Ambulances were not in evidence for the British. Before pushing off we were visited by a sort of propaganda officer who took photographs of us and pointed out that the British said that Germany did not have much air power – he drew our attention to this airfield which was crammed and very safely held. "Who is right?" he asked.

We started our road journey and burnt out tanks, damaged guns etc. marked the route where our companies had fought gallant fights to slow down the German advance. And some of the poor chaps had to go through the hell on Crete after that again, due to being evacuated to Crete.

On our arrival in the hospital we were met by Major Moore, an Australian and a dammed fine one at that who had voluntarily stayed behind on the evacuation of Greece. His manner was a tonic to us and after sorting out the bad cases and taking them in we were dispatched to the other camp, which was a sort of prison camp with hospital camp combined. We were given a mattress and two blankets and quartered in a wooden hut which had been a barrack room (I should have mentioned that we were in an old Greek barracks in the village of Kokkinia) and after some supplies lay down for the night. [This was Kokkinia Prisoner-of-War Hospital located above Piraeus.]

The next account moves on to describe in further detail what happened after the British evacuation left my father and others as prisoners of the Germans in firstly Crete, then Athens.

Herewith brief encounter of experience from the first day of the Battle of Crete. Wounded at Crete on the first day of the battle. (Shot between left shoulder and chest.)

8th day of the battle – the Germans discovered that the British were using a wireless in the hospital under cover of the Red Cross flag. This was perfectly true. The German commander did not ask questions, but mortar shelled the hospital, killing and wounding both British and German patients. I was wounded on the right shoulder during this incident. After the bombardment ceased, the German commander visited the hospital and sent for the Medical Officer [MO], Dr France, and warned him that it was against the rules of war and that if it happened again, he would blow the hospital to bits. "But", he said, "I'll accept your word as a British gentleman that the wireless will not open again".

The evacuation came as a surprise to the wounded and in my case a sickening feeling in the stomach at the thought of being a prisoner. At about 11 o'clock in the morning we were all informed that the British had evacuated and that we could now consider ourselves as prisoners. Private Walker of the Motor Transport [MT], well known as the water driver, informed me that he intended leaving as soon as they started to move us, which he did. A lot can be said for this man who was pretty badly wounded but showed no concern and was an inspiration to many by his happy-go-lucky attitude. I think Walker must have been the first of the wounded prisoners of Crete to escape.

The Germans in the hospital started looting the food and it was quite common to see them drinking tins of milk and eating tins of bully, which they seemed to have a mania for.

About a week later we were all moved to Heraklion Aerodrome to await air transport. A big German paratroop officer personally lifted all of us off the truck who could not jump for wounds. We lay about the aerodrome for nearly two days and some of the not so badly wounded took it in turns to watch Private Robertson who had been shot through the head and was continually trying to tear off his bandages.

(Private Robertson lived to reach the hospital and died about two weeks later from wounds.)

We were all transported to Greece by air and I found myself in a prison and hospital combined. I will not dwell on prison camp life as it is well known but will only mention the bagpipe incident. I should have mentioned before that I had retained my bagpipes all this time and as soon as I was reasonably better, I started to play them again. The Germans, except for a little show of interest, did not bother. Attached to our camp and about 600 yards away, was the main British hospital where the more serious cases were and, to break the monotony, both camps gave concerts. It was the custom of the hospital party to march down to us with a rag-time band and in a rag-time manner, which pleased the Germans.

Our Officer Commanding [OC], Doctor Moodie, then asked me if I would play our party through the village to the main hospital. I agreed and got the German OC's permission. At about 1700 hours our party formed up, including spectators. I then explained to them all, British, Australians, New Zealanders etc., in the following manner: "We are all British and we are going to march through the village to the pipes and I will not play unless you all assure me that you will put all you know into it and let the Germans see that although you may be POWs, you are not down".

I then made the party cover off in threes and with as loud a command as I could muster, moved the party to the right in threes, moved to the head of the column and gave the command, "By the right, quick march" and we moved off with the pipes playing. On the right wheeling at the gate, I could see that they were marching like Guardsmen and after marching about 100 yards we were stopped, and I was told not to play anymore, although the whole village had turned out to see us.

The following day, Captain Moodie asked for an explanation from the German OC and was told, "Play anything you like at any time except the Scottish flute". "Why not the Scottish flute?", Captain Moodie asked. "It excites your men too much", he was told.

I escaped from the camp on the 21st of July 1941 and managed to get my bagpipes over the barbed wire also. After the usual adventures connected with escaping, I managed to get out of Greece in a fishing boat on the 12th of September and reached the Turkish coast on the 15th of September. Travelled through Turkey to Syria, where by good luck 2nd Battalion were resting, and I managed to reach the battalion in time to be interviewed by Colonel G. A. Rusk, DSO, MC, just as the officers had finished dinner. The colonel insisted on opening a bottle of whisky to celebrate the occasion. So, ended my experience as a POW and before I close, I hope it will be understood that although the escape from the prison camp was done with no Greek assistance, I don't think getting out of Greece itself would have been so easy had it not been for so many brave and loyal Greek friends.

The following letter written by Brigadier Neil McMicking, OBE, DSC, MC of The Black Watch in December 1942 offers an account of the fighting experienced by The Black Watch during the Battle of Heraklion from the perspective of a German officer involved in the battle.

Major Burckhardt of the Lufftwaffen-Jäger-Brigade 1 was captured on the Alamein Front on November 5th, 1942.

He stated he was in command of a battalion of the

Air Division which, in company with two other battalions, made the parachute landing at Heraklion.

For some days beforehand, he had studied air photographs and intelligence reports of the objective he had to take, and he had come to the conclusion that there were no tanks, [Bren Gun] carriers, or A/A [anti-aircraft] guns to be reckoned with. For this reason, he took no A/Tk [anti-tank] weapons.

It had been intended that the parachute attack should be immediately preceded by a heavy Stuka raid in order to stun the defenders, but according to Burckhardt bad staff work crept in and the Stukas arrived far too early. . . at all events the defenders were not stunned. He maintains that owing to this the Bren Gunners were ready for him and he lost two of his JU52s before the men could jump.

When the battalion landed, they found not only half a dozen tanks waiting for them but also sixteen Bren Carriers. "The camouflage of these AFVs had been perfect. I had been sure when we jumped that we should have only infantry to deal with. That was my first surprise. The second was when I discovered who the infantry were."

No sooner had the parachutists landed than the infantry were upon them and so many of them were killed before they could get to the containers in which their arms were dropped. As soon as he could get a wireless set going Burckhardt asked for A/Tk weapons to be sent, but although these arrived, they were once again unable to reach the containers and few, if any, of the A/Tk weapons ever came into action. "The Jocks quickly grasped the importance of those little cylinders and seldom allowed us to come near them."

The battle continued with great ferocity for two days and the battalion suffered very heavy casualties.

"I had never expected such bitter fighting and we began to despair of ever gaining our objective, or indeed of surviving at all. The Bren Carriers were particularly dangerous to us, for they were not so blind as the tanks, and faster, and we had no armour piercing weapons. The only thing to do was to ambush and storm each one separately, jumping on them and killing the crew with machine pistols. They never surrendered. In this way we destroyed twelve carriers, but for each one I lost at least twenty men, sometimes more. Had it been any other regiment but The Black Watch – any other – all would have been well. Eventually we were at our wits' end. I had but 60 men left of my original 800, no food, little ammunition, and was no nearer success. The Jocks were eating our food. Next morning, I received the biggest surprise of an astonishing battle. They had all gone in the night."*

Although my father had described a considerable part of his experiences on Crete and mainland Greece, he never fully described the 'usual adventures connected with escaping', despite cajoling letters in 1947 from the then Brigadier Fergusson's assistant Betty Peirce at Combined Operations HQ in Kensington to send more detail for the brigadier's book about the history of The Black Watch. However, my father had described to him how he had walked out of the prison camp one night, taking advantage of the fact that he was unguarded after playing the pipes for the German officers, who, he said, regarded him as 'an unusually interesting trophy'. He walked out of the camp, out of the city and into the hills.

At this time, the walking wounded in the hospital and the fit prisoners in the prison camp were continually planning ways to escape. Amongst them was Captain Roy Farran (SAS) who had also

---

* Brigadier Neil McMicking, Company Commanders – Miscellaneous File, Letter No.1, 16 June 1944.

been captured in Crete. Contact had been made with Greeks willing to harbour prisoners and that summer an Australian and a New Zealander had escaped by pole-vaulting over the prison camp wire! In all, 26 other soldiers and officers escaped during a fierce stormy July night, leaving Farran behind to plan his own escape some time later. He described his mixed feelings of fury and delight on hearing of the escape which included my father, whom he described as 'my friend Robert, who left with his pipes in full marching order'.

Farran eventually escaped and reached the safe bungalow in Piraeus where he stayed for ten days with five other escaped prisoners, including my father, two Australians, a Polish Jew called George Filar, and a Palestinian called Christo. They were looked after by Madame Kareeyani. Writing about this period later in his book *Winged Dagger*, Farran said:

> [He was] much amused by the pains Pipe Major Roy took to preserve his other rank status. He frowned on attempts at familiarity, obviously believing that it was bad for discipline. The Greeks loved him.

Meanwhile, my uncle Neil received a letter dated August 1941 from Mrs J. K. Marsden on board the SS Cambion, sailing for New York, which said:

> It was on the 30th July that our party left Athens and we expect to be arriving in New York in a few days Tuesday August 29, I saw your brother when I was calling at a friend's house where he was being sheltered. He seemed to be well and was being cared for as well as could be in starving Athens. No one can foresee what might befall him and the many other English boys who are taking refuge in Greek homes. Your brother gave me your address and I promised to send you word of his well-being.

As the men planned various ways of escaping, they decided to split up into small groups, with Farran's group sailing via Crete towards Alexandria and my father's for Turkey, from where he would eventually reach Syria to re-join his regiment.

Fergusson wrote:

> For some days he was in company with the redoubtable Lieutenant (afterwards Major) Roy Farran, who had also escaped; but they parted, and it was Robert Roy who reached Salonika and eventually Turkey.

As my father stated, he would have been unable to have made his escape without the help of the Greek families who had looked after him. By 27th July 1941, wearing a suit of civilian clothes which had been procured for him and carrying forged papers, along with his English-Greek phrase book, he was picked up by a fishing boat, leaving behind his precious bagpipes with the Grafacos family with whom he had stayed with in Athens. His decision to leave them behind was informed by his assessment of the dangers that taking them would pose to others in his escape party. The fishing boat made a safe journey across the Aegean Sea to land its load of escapees and refugees in neutral Turkey where my father was soon on the road to Damascus in Syria. The Greeks had become true friends during this period.

On 16th September 1941, an 'Emergency Certificate' was issued to my father by the British Consulate General, Smyrna (Turkey) authorising his journey to Syria, Palestine, and Egypt, leaving Izmir by train via Ankara.

From Turkey, my father wrote to a friend he named Pipie, describing his escape on the evening.

> [A] storm was blowing, and the moon did not rise until 12 midnight, so you can understand that I got well away in spite of the fact there was a curfew from 12 midnight until 5 am. I lay down on the hillside for a

couple of hours sleep with four others who escaped with me. In the morning when we woke up, we found that about 200 yards below us was a German ordnance camp and to the extreme right of the village an ack-ack gun, so we had to be very wary in our movements. At about 2 pm one of the men took ill from exposure to the sun and lack of water, so I went down the other side of the hill for water and being in uniform was ready to expect anything from hostile Greeks to perhaps a German post. Imagine my surprise when almost the whole village welcomed me and treated me like some hero; anyway, as the welcome was so good, I brought my friends down and we were given food, cigarettes and had our wounds attended to where necessary and at night moved secretly to a home. I might mention I escaped with my silver mounted bagpipes! After two days we were moved to Athens by wealthier Greeks and put in separate houses to await an opportunity of getting a boat.

During his stay in the Athens safe house he wrote to a friend.

My time I devoted to collecting information and am happy to say made a fairly good job before sailing for Turkey in a large fishing boat on the 12th of September, so at the time of writing I am in Turkey and move to-morrow, 20th September for Egypt. If you receive letters which are mysterious don't bother about them as they were smuggled out before I got away. I intend to write to you when I reach British territory so one or the other will reach you, so tell my people that I am safe and well and more or less better and fit for action on the field again.

My father also described in this letter his resolution to make his escape from the outset.

I often thought as I made my plans and arrangements to escape that this was the sort of adventure you would have enjoyed as a young man.

In 1944, a postcard was sent to my father from Lydia Prousaers of 9 St Vasiliou Street, Athens. It was written on 9th June 1944 but only reached my father towards the end of July 1945. It not only demonstrates a close friendship but also gives a hint of the hardships faced by the Greeks during the occupation.

Dear Bob

Today I had a telephone call from Betty giving me the delightful news of the arrival of your letter to the Grocer. Can you imagine our delight when after four years of hardships and suffering we again are all free and able to hear good news from our dear friend? Very often Betty and I speak about you and remember how thoughtful you were about us, the only real friend who appreciated our efforts and sacrifices.

I went to the prison in May 1942 and came out on Christmas 1942. Betty and my younger sister went too, but I, being more naughty, stayed longer. I stayed in the dungeon for more than a week and I was isolated for more than a month but thank God everything is over. Kazajami was killed some months before we were free. The Germans killed her. All the rest of the friends you met are well. Frank [Robert Roy's brother-in-law] was the first Englishman I set eyes on when the first day we were free, but unfortunately, he wasn't as friendly as one would expect him to be. If you ever come to Greece, we will have to tell you a lot of things. Donald, that tall thin chap at Farios came back and stayed with them for ten days. Do come and visit us when you can. Much love to you Bob, write soon.

Shortly after the first postcard, a second postcard arrived from Domisios Grafacos, 250 Patisia Street, Athens.

> Dear friend Robert
> We are well. I sent you this short letter and I hope that it will find you quite well. If you are in England please you to reply me because I want to know about your health. If you are not in England please somebody of your family to send me your address because during the war, I kept him (father's bagpipes) here in Athens in my house. He must be quiet that his favourite play is in our house and it is waiting him. My children are always thinking about you, privately the little Helena. Many compliments to your family. I miss you. All the best.

Another letter was sent by Lydia Prousaers to Cath Glennie in Aboyne, who in November 1945 wrote to my father.

> Dear (Pipe) Major Roy
> I had a letter recently from Lydia Prousaers with some snaps which she asked me to send on to you. The address she gave seems rather inadequate, but I trust this will find you all right.
> It must be grand for you to be home (if you still are) after all you went through in Greece.
> Life is still very strenuous there and prices are exorbitant, and I don't know how people live at all. Lydia seems to be rather tired and no wonder after so much privation.

The silver-mounted bagpipes left behind in Athens were kept safely there until his brother-in-law Frank Owens, then a demobbed sapper in Greece, collected and returned them to Scotland. Frank, as Lydia Prousaers's letter of 9th June 1944 shows, did not make the same positive impression on the families however.

PHOTOGRAPH
SECTION

1

BEGINNINGS, PALESTINE, CRETE, GREECE, AND SYRIA

1—Agnes Roy (*née* Riddell).

2—No. 2 Section, F Company, the 2nd Battalion, The Black Watch, India, 1898.
William Roy, second row, third from left.

3—All India Hockey Tournament, Allahabad, India, 1900. Winner: The Black Watch.

4—Robert Roy, The Black Watch, centre.

5—Rutherglen Pipe Band, Largs War Memorial. Robert Roy, sixth from right.

6—Presentation of new Colours to the 2nd Battalion, The Black Watch, Balmoral Castle, 14th September 1937. Robert Roy on far left.

7—Christmas/New Year card from Jerusalem, Palestine, 1937 or 1938.

8—Pipe Band, Jerusalem, Palestine.

9—In Palestine or India. Robert Roy on right.

10—Decorative brass plate commemorating the service of the 2nd Battalion, The Black Watch, Palestine, 1937-9, formerly belonging to Corporal W. S. Latto of the Battalion's Signals Section. Black Watch Museum (A5739 – on display).

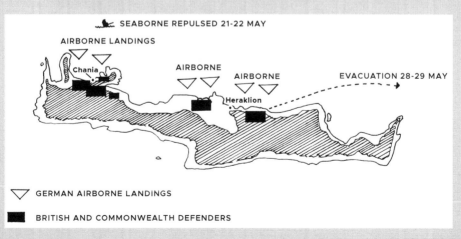

11—Battle for Crete, May-June 1941.

12—Infantry Record Office notification of wounding of 2216942 Pipe Major Robert Roy, 29th August 1941.

29

13—Christmas card from Crete, 1941. Robert Roy, centre.

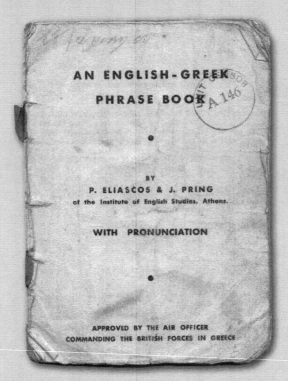

14—Robert Roy's English-Greek phrase book.

15—Members of the Greek family who hid Robert Roy, on right.

16—Members of the Greek family who hid Robert Roy.

17—Robert Roy in civilian clothes during his escape from Athens.

18—Forged ID card used to escape from Greece.

EMERGENCY CERTIFICATE   № 78

THIS IS TO CERTIFY THAT *Mr Robert ROY*

has stated to me that he is a *British Subject by Birth* and that I have no reason to doubt his statement.

This Certificate is valid only for the journey to *Syria, Palestine and Egypt* leaving Izmir *by train via Ankara*

Signature of bearer:

R Roy

and must be surrendered to the proper authority on arrival at destination.

Given at H.B.M. Consulate-General, Smyrna, this *16* day of *September* 1941.

B. *[signature]*
H.B.M. CONSUL-GENERAL.

19—Emergency Travel Certificate given
to Robert Roy at H.B.M. Consulate-General, Smyrna,
16th September 1941, to aid travel through Syria.

CHAPTER 3

SYRIA TO TOBRUK

BY THE SUMMER of 1941, General Wavell, Commander-in-Chief Middle East, had three campaigns underway, but with limited resources. A Middle East force had to be deployed to Iraq, an abortive attack known as 'Battleaxe' was ordered for the Western Desert, and the build-up of the Axis forces in Syria could not be ignored. One British battalion (the 2nd Battalion, The Black Watch) alone was left as part of the garrison in the River Nile Delta.

Second Battalion moved off on 7th July and for a while was based near Zahlé, a small town in the eastern foothills of Mount Lebanon. On 19th August, Lieutenant Colonel George Archer Rusk arrived to take over command. Training went on, interspersed with relaxation. In this area, there was no immediate crisis so there was time to train the reinforcements, recuperate, and improve fitness. It was into this base that my father appeared after his escape from Crete. He walked unannounced, dressed in blue coat and grey flannel trousers into the lines, reporting back for duty. After the celebratory whisky, he resumed his position as pipe major.

The first warning of the impending move, not yet known, came on 18th September. Most knew it had to be Tobruk, which since 4th April had been held by the 9th Australian Division which had been defending the port against Italian and German attacks in the extraordinarily harsh environment and often unbearable heat of the Tobruk day. The Australian government had insisted the time had come for its relief.

An advance party left on 19th September, though the main body did not follow for another month. By the time the battalion left on 19th October, the Scots and Australians were firm friends. The journey to Tobruk was hazardous and when the 2nd Battalion reached Tobruk's harbour there was continual fire in progress. The ships berthed side-by-side adjacent to a wreck which served as a pier and the men walked across the intervening pontoon to the shore. Trucks then took them to a spot four miles from the harbour, which was the reserve brigade area – Fort Pilastrino.

The 2/4th (Battalion) Australians, who were due to leave two days later, held a handing over ceremony, which was recorded for broadcasting to the Australian network. At this point, no pipes were played, much to my father's disappointment, though this was justified as preventing the enemy knowing the composition of the garrison and that a relief had taken place. But it would not be long before they were played again with a vengeance.

Around 29th October, the battalion moved up to the actual perimeter and gradually established their routine patrolling every night. Water was scarce and barely drinkable; the diet was largely corned beef, tinned fish, and biscuits. Day after day, Tobruk was plagued with dust storms and every night constant air raids thundered over the harbour, usually until 10 pm. After dark, the ration convoys would come, and the arrival of a wireless broke the grinding routine, bringing news to the soldiers. There was also a daily news sheet, the Tobruk News, which really only repeated the news already heard on the wireless.

Rumours were rife about a major 'push' from Egypt to attempt to break the siege, which would also involve the 70th Division inside Tobruk breaking out and joining up with the 8th Army. On 7th November, the 2nd Battalion was withdrawn from the perimeter knowing that it would have a leading role in the impending battle. The garrison was to await the code word 'Pop', which would signify time for action and that the enemy was on the run. However, none had realised that Generalleunant Erwin Rommel, commander of the German Afrika Korps, had also chosen this very same date to deploy his best troops and equipment to disperse the allied troops heading towards Tobruk.

On the evening of 20th November, the long-awaited signal came, and the 2nd Battalion moved off. Behind them the usual air raid was going on over the harbour and out in front of no-man's-land. The three infantry battalions leading the breakout moved to the area manned by the 2nd Leicesters who were preparing the front for the breakout. At 6.30 am they began their attack, but most tanks and Bren Gun Carriers were disabled by mines. The 2nd Battalion, King's Own Regiment (Lancaster), with fixed bayonets, secured position 'Butch', but at great cost, with 30 dead and over 70 casualties; and then moved forward to 'Jill', a position which was wired and heavily mined.

The time had come for The Black Watch to enter the fray. B Company (The Black Watch) advanced with bayonets fixed. However, things went wrong from the outset. The guns of the Royal Horse Artillery were to fire on 'Jill', but the tanks meant to support the advance did not arrive on time. B Company moved off knowing they did not have this support. The tanks arrived four minutes late but then crossed the wrong bridge and set off into no-man's land. They quickly realised their mistake and changed direction.

Meanwhile, B Company had advanced for several hundred yards without incident but were then attacked ferociously. As the battle raged, there were many casualties including the deaths of three of B Company's five officers, and the loss of seven of the company's thirteen NCOs. Many of the casualties were caused by fire from two German machine guns hidden in sage bushes. Position 'Tiger' was the next target, yet there were still no tanks with which to lead an assault. Nonetheless, one B Company officer and ten men pushed on.

B Company's rapid advance had left many pockets of resistance. Into this arena came D Company with the other companies following on behind. German machine guns, shells, mortars, and small arms fire caused havoc as enemy fire cut swathes into the advancing battalion which unruffled pressed on. In the midst of this rose the sound of the pipes played by my father and Pipe Sergeant McNicoll. They played *Hielan' Laddie* (the regimental quick march of The Black Watch), *Lawson's Men*, and *The Black Bear*, urging on the battle-fatigued men towards the enemy positions. These tunes sounded over the field and one officer who was badly wounded in the arm and leg wrote afterwards:

> I would say that the Pipe Major's playing was
> instrumental in kindling the spirit with which the
> whole attack was carried out. I heard *Highland
> Laddie* as I lay in 'Jill' and it was the tune that got me
> back on my feet and advancing again.

Traditionally being conducive in raising morale and encouraging extra effort in the heat of battle, the sound of the bagpipes inspires Scottish soldiers. The enemy, all too aware of their impact that day, inevitably targeted the two Black Watch pipers. My father was shot repeatedly but nevertheless continued to get back on his feet and play. After being shot three times, he was unable to raise himself but carried on playing on the ground. Many years later, James McGraw, then a lance corporal, drummer, and non-commissioned officer (NCO) in Pipe Major Roy's company, said:

> There we were, waiting for zero hour. We were all in a
> long straight line and when the advances started 'Rab'
> started playing. He was leading the battalion in when
> one of the first hail of bullets must have hit him. He
> dropped and got up. Then he was hit again and again
> – he got up, the pipes still under his arm. When he
> could not get up, he still played lying on the ground.

Pipe Sergeant McNicoll played on as my father was carried back to the regimental aid post for treatment. There, clad in bandages, he continued to pipe to the other wounded, to the astonishment of a captured German medical officer who was dressing the wounds of British soldiers.

At 9 am, the tanks joined the battle and began dealing with the machine guns, while the infantry went for the anti-tank guns. Prisoners, who soon totalled nearly 500, began surrendering everywhere. However, the 2nd Battalion had lost six officers and 58 men; 196 were wounded, fifteen fatally. It had been a fierce battle, which though fought bravely, had incurred dreadful loss.

The first casualty at Tobruk occurred on 30th October: Major Sir Colin K. Dick Cunyngham, aged 33, was mortally wounded when an anti-tank mine exploded under a ration truck as he was standing on its running board. Later, on 21st November, Sergeant Andrew Scobie, Captain Mellon, and 2nd Lieutenant Cromarty were killed between 'Jill' and 'Jack'. Second Lieutenant P. Hill and Company Sergeant Major Scott had remained at the 'Observation Post' to disperse and direct men and became easy targets: Hill was wounded, and Scott killed.

These officer casualties happened at the same time my father was wounded three times. Major Andy A. Pitcairn, who had served in Crete with my father, and Captain Archie E. D. Wilder were also killed at this point in the battle. Although 'Tiger' was fully held by 10.15 am, there remained then few functioning officers – Colonel G. A. Rusk, Captain Boyle, Captain Ewan, and Lieutenant D. C. Menzies among them. By the end of the battle, nine officers and 96 men had been killed in action.

The 'Roll of Honour' of the 2nd Battalion, The Black Watch, shows the tremendous loss at Tobruk.

Bernard Fergusson who arrived in Tobruk ten days after the battle stated:

> I have never had such an onset of pride in the regiment as when, guided by my cousin Richard Boyle, I saw what they had done that morning of 21 November.

A major of the Royal Horse Artillery who saw the whole action wrote:

> I class this attack of The Black Watch as one of the most outstanding examples of gallantry combined with high-class training that I have ever seen. Not one of us there will ever forget such supreme gallantry.

My father was awarded the Distinguished Conduct Medal (DCM)

on 21st November 1941. The citation read:

> On 21 November 1941 Pipe Major Roy displayed the most exceptional and outstanding gallantry and devotion to duty in the attack of the Battalion on TIGER from the Tobruk perimeter. From the start line to the German Battalion position commanding the objective, he played his pipes with the foremost troops almost continuously throughout the advance of 2.5 miles, under heavy enemy fire of all kinds for the entire distance.
>
> When collective movement ceased, and while the enemy position was being reduced, the Pipe Major crawled round to the wounded men near him, dressing wounds and giving them water, when any movement brought down a hail of enemy fire.
>
> In the vicinity of the objective he was ordered back to the RAP having been wounded three times. His bravery and example of complete disregard of personal danger was an inspiration to the advancing troops and had a direct bearing on maintaining the impetus of the attack.
>
> This NCO previously distinguished himself in the defence of Crete where he was again wounded and captured by the enemy. On recovery he escaped from a POW camp in Greece and at considerable personal danger made his way to Syria where he rejoined the Battalion.

News of the battle reached Britain.

In Perthshire, *The People's Journal* of Saturday, 6th December asked, 'Who is the gallant piper of Tobruk?' Relatives and friends were quoted as saying that the action of 'The Piper of Tobruk' 'is just the sort of thing he would do'. His sister Mary said she was convinced he was her brother Robert. Friends of my father in Dunfermline also confirmed this, saying he and their son were in the same regiment.

The Scotsman headlined with 'Tobruk Piper, Gallant Glasgow Man, His name revealed' and reported:

> The gallant Scots Piper of Tobruk who, though wounded, refused to stop playing, is Pipe Major Robert Roy of Glasgow. Numerous messages of inquiry and congratulation have been received by his sister Mrs James Wilson who revealed to a representative of *The Scotsman* last night that her brother had apparently had many exciting experiences in the past six months. Highlanders advancing from Tobruk, it was stated, towards the end of last month, captured five strongholds at the bayonet point, cut up a German infantry battalion and captured its commanding officer. To achieve this, they had to advance forwards with fixed bayonets. It was Pipe Major Roy who played them into action. Mrs Wilson said, "We read the story in the papers about 'The Piper of Tobruk'. Friends in various parts of Scotland must have read the story too, for they sent us cuttings from the newspapers and suggested it was Robert. Then came a War Office message saying that Robert had been wounded and was in a Middle East field hospital". Mrs Wilson explained that her brother learned to play the pipes at the age of 14 when he joined the works pipe band of Stewarts and Lloyds Ltd. When 16 he joined The Black Watch. Robert is the eldest of a family of six. Their parents are dead. A younger brother, Neil, was with Robert in Palestine, in The Black Watch, when war was declared. Pipe Major Roy was for a long time one of the unhappiest men inside Tobruk. He had his pipes but was not allowed to play lest the strains of Scottish airs should give the enemy a clue to the composition of the garrison. The Pipe Major has a notable record of

gallantry. Captured in the Battle of Crete he was flown to Greece, but escaped from a German prison camp, chartered a fishing boat, reaching Syria and eventually rejoined his regiment. His original pipes lie in the house of some faithful Greek friends, who have promised to return them after the war. The second set lay unused in a dug-out, waiting for the great moment when he piped his men to victory on Tobruk's perimeter.

'We'll Harry the Hun' was another headline of the day. The accompanying article stating:

Much more deadly than the attacks in Libya and on the Don is the blow struck by the people of Britain this week. Never before has the world seen anything like the new conscription measure. Hitler needn't bleat that this is the latest act of tyranny by the Government on the people. Another two and a quarter million men will be in the battle as a result of the age limit being lowered to 18 and a half and raised from 41 to 51.

The *Perthshire People's Journal* of 6th December 1941 also headlined my father's bravery alongside another article entitled 'Carry Your Gas Mask Next Time', which described the first official gas exercise in Scotland being carried out in Perth. This covered normally busy streets such as High Street, St John's Street, South Street, and Methven Street.

[M]any of the public who came out after the finish found to their great disadvantage that the gas remained in the affected area for a considerable time, and tears were shed for a number of hours afterwards by people who walked in the contaminated areas. The streets were described as having 'pea soup fog' once tear gas had been let off.

The driver of a horse-drawn cart in George Inn Lane was a bit perplexed when the rattles sounded. Donning his own mask, he drew up the horse and pulled off his jacket and tied it tightly round his horse's head in an attempt to protect the animal from the gas. His efforts were hardly necessary as tear gas does not affect animals to a great extent, but his humane efforts to save his charge were well looked upon by the people round about.

Tucked away in this same newspaper was the poignant announcement in the death columns of a 26-year-old soldier who died of wounds in the Middle East, leaving behind his young Perthshire wife.

The Glasgow Herald of 1st December 1941 criticised what appeared to be the general discouragement of Scottish music by the BBC! Writing about my father's bravery and the fact he was not allowed to play his pipes at first, *The Glasgow Herald* stated:

What is most remarkable is the maintenance of this grand record at a time when, far from being fostered, the distinctive customs of the Highland Regiment have sometimes seemed to be rather heavily frowned upon. The story of the Tobruk piper throws a not wholly flattering light on the working of the military mind, feeling that this has been yet another occasion where a staff passion for official secrecy has been allowed to stand in the way of a matter of real military importance – the maintenance of Regimental morale under peculiarly trying conditions.

The Illustrated London News of 20th December 1941 published photographs of the Libyan battle scenes, showing pictures of the battle and 'the terrain where the Imperial forces first launched a full-scale offensive against the Axis army'. The photograph shows my father playing his pipes to both British and German wounded soldiers and the wounded of both sides. The caption read:

> Some light relief after the battle: while British wounded
> and wounded enemy await medical attention by British
> and enemy Red Cross orderlies, a Highland Regiment
> piper entertains them with his pipes.

However, other newspapers of the time were more selective in their publishing, choosing to omit the section of the photo showing the German wounded.

In Egypt, on Sunday, 11th January 1942, a memorial service was held for those who fell in action at Tobruk between October and December 1941. The chaplain of the battalion, the Reverend W. L. Cochrane gave a poignant address.

> Two and a half years of war and the goal is not reached
> yet. Though much of the finest blood in the Empire has
> been spilled we seem to have still a long way to go. A
> few months ago, this battalion went to the Western
> Desert to serve the common cause.
>
> We have returned from there again and those of us
> here today are thankful for the health and strength
> that are ours. But our ranks are thinned. Many officers
> and men have made the supreme sacrifice. There are
> friends whom we shall never again take by the right
> hand; comrades whose good company we shall never
> again enjoy. What shall we say of the part they have
> played, we shall say "they have written a fresh chapter
> in the history of the Regiment and they have written it
> in fair lines". And when that better world order comes
> for which they have given their all, a better world order
> which, alas, they were not spared to see and enjoy,
> what will be the judgement of men? The judgement of
> men will be the judgement of God. Forasmuch as it
> was in their hearts, they did well that it was in their
> hearts.

On 16th April 1942, my father received a letter from Jenkinson Bowerstall. He wrote:

> We had a letter from Millie yesterday, saying you were the means of saving Jimmy's life. I don't know what to say and how to thank you, but you will understand that we feel you deserve the VC. Millie says you have received the DCM. You are a brave lad.

In December of that year, my father was awarded 'The Oak Leaf Emblem' by King George VI.

———————

CHAPTER 4

INDIA

THE 2ND BATTALION, The Black Watch, returned to Syria to be re-fitted and rested. Then on 7th December 1942, the Japanese Air Force struck Pearl Harbour and the men of The Black Watch were on the move again – off on troopships through the Suez Canal, bound for Rangoon, Burma. Rangoon fell while they were still at sea, so they were diverted to Bombay, India. From there, the units were sent to various camps in the Deccan Plateau (that stretches across western and southern India), with the Battalion then being sent to Ranchi in the state of Jharkhand (eastern India), where it re-joined Divisional HQ and another brigade of 70th Division.

During this time in India, a young Berwickshire piper, Tim Ainslie, joined the 2nd Battalion, where he became part of my father's piping cadre and began a devotion to piping that would never leave him. (Pipe Major Tim Ainslie later went on to teach many pipers, including Pipe Major Steven Small, who became director of bagpipe music for the British Army.)

India at the time was witnessing internal troubles, the worst of which came in Bihar and Bengal, and troops were sent out frequently to these places to maintain public order. By this time, the monsoon was beginning, and a huge cyclone hit Midnapore (West Bengal) in October 1942. The entire area was flooded, and scenes of desolation emerged, with no houses left standing, ships carried inland, and dead bodies everywhere. The Battalion spent weeks helping the local people, organising shelter, and supplies for both the battalion and civilians. The horrific impact of the cyclone and its aftermath successfully settled the unrest in Midnapore, where the people said they would never forget what the men of The Black Watch (Royal Highland Regiment) had done for them.

Support for the Indian people affected by the cyclone was shown in various forms during their time there. The bagpipes continued to play a major part of The Black Watch regimental life and also contributed to events held by charitable organisations. For example, on Sunday, 2nd August 1942, a grand concert was organised in aid of The Lady Mary Herbert's Bengal Women's War Fund, with 'the full pipe band of a Famous Scottish Regiment' headlining the programme. This was held at the New Empire, 'India's Premier Playhouse' with the permission of Colonel G. A. Rusk, and with the pipes and drums under my father. Not only was the full range of reels, strathspeys, and marches played but also a variety of dances took place, including sword dances, foursome reels, and highland flings.

In September 1943, while in camp near Bangalore (in the state of Karnataka), the Battalion was informed by Lieutenant-Colonel Green, who had succeeded Colonel Rusk in May, that the 70th Division was to be converted into Chindits.* Their role would be to penetrate the enemy's lines in Burma and the Battalion was to be re-organised and replaced by 'Columns', comprising around 400 men, including a reconnaissance platoon supported by Burmese hill tribesmen. The senior of the 2nd Battalion's two columns, 73 Column, was commanded by Lieutenant-Colonel George Green and the second, 42 Column, by Major David Rose.

The decision to convert 70th Division had been made by Winston Churchill at a conference in Quebec and all were expected to accept the changes. There was considerable disappointment that the Division was to lose its identity and be broken up. There remained only one company of men, who were due for repatriation after six years of foreign service. My father, who had more than completed his term overseas, was repatriated to Britain. Just before leaving, he was referred to the Royal Army Medical Corps as his wounds continued to cause discomfort. Captain D. C. Langwell, the 2nd Battalion, The Black Watch, India Command, wrote to his colleague Sandy, saying:

---

* Commando troops led by General Orde Wingate in Burma.

This is just a note introducing CSM Roy to you. I wonder if you remember me as a medical student. Wilson Harrington and I attended our first post mortem in the Royal when you were doing them. Also used to meet you at dances etc. Well, the story is something like this: Roy got badly shot in Crete through the chest and since then has had a certain amount of pain. This has increased lately, and I didn't want to send him into a hospital out here for investigation as he is due to go home within two or three days. I would be very pleased if you would look at him and tell him exactly what you think about it.

———————

CHAPTER 5

GERMANY

MY FATHER duly arrived back in Scotland but after six months in Britain, he had the urge to be off again and volunteered for further duty overseas. He was posted to the 7th Battalion, The Black Watch, and joined them at Vught in the Netherlands in October 1944. Almost simultaneously he received the letter from Grafacos in Athens, regarding his bagpipes, which were then collected by his brother-in-law Frank Owens.

The anniversary of El Alamein was on 23rd October and seen to be an appropriate day for the beginning of the main advance towards Hertogenbosch. The 7th Battalion moved off at 11.15 am to seize a bridge over a small river at Sint-Michielsgestel (southern Netherlands). Although the bridge was blown up before troops reached it, a platoon successfully formed a way across and by daybreak, most of the 1st and the 7th Battalion, The Black Watch, were across the river with armour and anti-tank guns. 7th Battalion moved on and captured around 200 prisoners, including some 'Green Police' from the notorious concentration camp at Vught.

From there, 154 Brigade, with 1st and 7th Battalion, pushed on as far as Gertruidenburg and Raamsdonk, while the 5th Battalion headed northwards to Hertogenbosch. By November 1944, the area between Maastricht and Nijmegen remained to be cleared out. The 5th went to Weert, the 7th to Ospel, and the 1st to Leveroy. By the end of the month, Baarlo was liberated by the 1st Battalion, and the next focus became the area west of the German/Dutch frontier – areas susceptible to flooding around Nijmegen and Arnhem. The warning to beware of flooding was sent to all troops.

5th Battalion was near Opheusden, the 1st at Valburg and 7th at Andelst. On 3rd December 1944, the 1st Battalion found itself in the front-line when the Seaforth Highlanders and Queen's Own

Cameron Highlanders of 152 Brigade were expelled by mounting floods. Two companies of 7th Battalion had to fall back on the 4th of December, and a third on the 5th. At Zetten, 5th and 7th Battalion had supplies delivered by boat, but there were still German troops in the village and any movement was dangerous.

On 19th December, the wireless announced the beginning of the German offensive in the Ardennes involving a difficult move through bitter weather. On 6th January 1945, the fighting peaked and on 7th January, the Highland Division was moved to the west; following up the retreating army for ten days. After this, other formations poured in from every direction and by 22nd January, all battalions were back to those areas they had been sent from 30 days earlier.

The Highland Division then operated in the southern Reichswald area or in the forested area lying to the south and south-east of Reichswald. The Siegfried Line ran through Reichswald Forest from north to south. Although it was hoped that this would be a short battle, the wet weather, deliberate flooding, and the postponed American assault prevented such a result.

The River Rhine and River Maas water levels were high and there were problems with the lines of communication. There were only two bridges across the Maas into the Nijmegen bridgehead from where the attack was to start and these had to be used by eight divisions, which took time to organise. 154 Brigade crossed after dark on 6th February. The following day was spent in last minute preparations and on the 8th at 5 am, over 1,000 guns fired continuously until 1 pm.

The attack was led by 1st and 7th Battalion. The latter was on the right and had a flank open towards the River Maas. Their objectives were a few hundred yards short of the forest. 7th Battalion succeeded in two of these objectives but was hit by snipers who killed the company commander Major Lowe and two of his platoon commanders, before being dealt with by tanks. First Battalion achieved its objective in the forest and was the first to reach German ground.

Next day, the two Black Watch battalions remained where they were while 5th Battalion began to head south. Then the move proceeded to the heart of the Siegfried Line, with 7th Battalion going for the small village of Villers, which it soon occupied; and took many prisoners. On the 16th, the 1st Battalion successfully attacked the railway station at Hassum, supported by 'Crocodiles'* belonging to a squadron of the Fife and Forfar Yeomanry.

The next target was Goch, where 5th and 7th Battalion engaged in a fierce attack with heavy enemy shelling. 7th Battalion was now put under 153 Brigade, which had been weakened by this time. Both battalions remained in and around Goch for a week, recuperating and reorganising, during which time Winston Churchill came to visit and watch the 'Pipes and Drums' play *Retreat*. On 7th/8th March, the Brigade moved south again to the area of Roermond to prepare for the crossing of the Rhine.

The Northampton Yeomanry had supported 154 Brigade throughout the fighting in Europe and had returned now fully trained in using 'Buffalos' to help carry the 1st and 7th Battalions across the Rhine. Advance parties of 154 Brigade were sent forward and at 5 pm on 22nd March, the artillery programme began.

The 7th Argyll and Sutherland Highlanders and 7th Battalion were the first to go on the Buffalos and crossed a mile short of the Rhine on a perfect moonlit night at 9 pm. One Buffalo was blown up, but there was no shelling or small arms fire until they reached the shore. 7th Battalion was proud to have been the first to cross. The 1st Battalion followed an hour and a half later heading for Speldrop and Klein Esserden, but soon ran into trouble. Major Richard Boyle, who had served with my father in Crete and Tobruk, was killed on the outskirts of Klein Esserden, where there were deep minefields and a strong defence. The enemy was still holding out the next day, but by 10 am tanks finally arrived and cleared Klein Esserden. The Brigade then proceeded to Speldrop, but their attack failed. By 8 pm, however, a fresh battalion of Canadian troops had cleared the village after furious fighting.

---

* Tanks with flame-throwing equipment.

The 5th Battalion, The Black Watch, had crossed upstream, immediately west of Rees, and with the Gordons Highlanders proceeded to Esserden. The Gordon Highlanders however, were held up at Rees and 5th Battalion was sent to attack. The fighting went on all night and all next morning. On the 26th, 7th Battalion was to make a bridgehead for the Guards Armoured Division to break out. The leading company of the battalion advanced at 9.30 pm and reached the bridge that had been prepared for demolition, but as they were about to cross, fierce firing ensued, preventing any crossing. At this stage, no one knew that a small group of survivors was on the other side: Lieutenant-Colonel McBride with five of his men were hiding, with some wounded troops, in a house overlooking the crossing.

At dawn, when eight German soldiers crawled up to blow up the bridge, McBride's group attacked them, killing the officer and two others; the rest surrendered. During the next two days, Dinxperlo was overcome and on 30th March the Guards Armoured Division was underway. The rest of the story is well documented – the Allies rapidly crossed Germany, still encountering battles as they went until the final surrender of the German Army in May 1945.

The British were to retain control of North Germany, apart from the area around Bremerhaven, which was assigned to the Americans. My father's platoon was based firstly at Hesedorf, close to the Germans' supply camp and notorious Herzogenbusch Concentration Camp. This was the only camp run directly by the SS in Western Europe outside of Germany and was first used in 1943; holding 31,000 prisoners, of whom 749 died there. The camp's prisoners were transferred to other camps shortly before the camp was liberated in 1944.

A reporter for *The Glasgow Weekly News* wrote a graphic description of what life was like there for the soldiers of The Black Watch, which was published in the newspaper on Sunday, 8th December 1944. The war correspondent met my father at Hesedorf and wrote about their first meeting.

One evening, just as it was getting dark, I was attracted by the skirl of the pipes from a little wood behind some of the huts. Walking among the trees to investigate I came upon one of the young pipers being put through his paces.

After the lesson had been completed and the pupil had made a good job of playing *Highland Laddie*, which is The Black Watch regimental March, the instructor introduced himself as RSM Robert Roy and invited me over to his billet for a chat.

"You're the newspaper reporter, aren't you?" he asked. I admitted I was doing my best to live up to that description. "Come on then," he said, "and I'll give you a story...".

And, by jings, he did! My father told him all about the Regiment's involvement over the war years, including Crete and Tobruk and the bagpipes he had finally regained. The war correspondent then realised the extent to which a Highland regiment values its men and its piping.

The Black Watch feel a bit cut off from the outer world in their camp in the heart of a country district of Germany. It was pretty lonely there when I was with them some weeks ago. It will be lonelier now that the snow is falling, and the fields and roads are becoming ice-bound. But as long as the pipes keep playing the old familiar tunes the Jocks have a grand link with home.

You usually waken at Hesedorf to the skirl of the pipes, and at various times throughout the day, right on till after dark, there is one of the battalion pipers, or one of the young soldiers who is ambitious to become a member of the band, playing or practising in some odd corner of the camp.

Those of you who have been to Dunoon on a Cowal Games day will have some idea of the atmosphere. You know what a peculiar thrill it is to hear the pipes as you step off the boat which has brought you from Gourock. You can imagine how much bigger a thrill it is to have the silence broken by the sound of bagpipes and to think – "Yes, this is Germany, but it's also a wee corner of Scotland!"

There's something bitter-sweet about the pipes. They cheer you up and make you feel a little bit homesick at the same time. This was impressed upon me in a way I'll never forget when I attended a Guest Night in the Officers' Mess.

There were eight or nine visitors from neighbouring units and a company of 27 sat down to tackle the following menu: hors d'oeuvres, tomato soup, roast wild duck, pheasant and chicken, roast potatoes, carrots and peas, peach melba, and angels on horseback.

After we had toasted the King, we settled down to a programme played by Pipe Major Anderson of Dundee and two of the regimental pipers – all looking very braw in their full-dress regalia.

First of all, there was the 'Piobaireachd', *The Lament for Glengarry* played by the pipe major himself. We sat with bowed heads as he paced round and round. I lost count of the number of times he circled the big dining room. The drone of the pipes, wailing out their slow lament, turned my mind to thoughts of those who had given their lives for their country. The whole thing became an ordeal. I still recall the tremendous feeling of relief when the music stopped, and the lament was ended.

For a few minutes there was dead silence. The conversation resumed in hushed voices and the CO called for the pipe major who reappeared from a little side room and drank the traditional half tumbler of whisky.

The next item, by the three pipers, was a slow march, *My Home*, which brought a change of atmosphere. Oppressive sorrow was replaced by homesickness as the listeners remembered parents and wives and children and other loved ones so many hundreds of miles away over the North Sea.

Then, in quick succession came a march, *The Duke of Roxburgh's Farwell to Blackmount Forest*, a Strathspey, *Maggie Cameron*, and a reel, *Duntroon*. The majestic martial music made me think with pride of the part played by these men of the Highland Division on the long road to victory.

Having gone through all the changing emotions from sadness to joy, we finished up with our feet tapping time to the reel. Then tables and chairs were pushed aside and some of the officers entertained the company with *Strip the Willow* and the *Eightsome Reel*. I was surprised to learn that The Black Watch officers have regular dancing classes, at which the CO himself acts as instructor.

It struck me a queer idea until I was reminded that it would be a bad show if a Highland officer at a formal ball had to confess, he couldn't do a Highland dance. He must not only be able to take part, but he must know every step and part. How very different was the graceful reel I saw at Hesedorf from the rowdy hotch-potch of hooching and birling which passes for an eightsome in these modern days of jive and jitterbugs in the Scottish dance halls!

––––––––––

CHAPTER 6

DUISBURG

BY MARCH 1945, General Eisenhower had declared the Ruhr cities a 'death zone' which had to be left immediately. Heavy bombing continued over the entire area (before the war ended two months later), leaving most of the cities including the region's important inland port of Duisburg destroyed.

In December 1945, the men of the 51st Highland Division held their Highland Games at Verden Stadium near Bremen. Nine massed bands played in a grand finale under my father. By 1946, the 1st Battalion was based in Glamorgan Barracks, Duisburg, followed by the 2nd Battalion. On 13th July 1948, both battalions were amalgamated there.

In Duisburg, my father was billeted in a house, a former Beamtenhauser (civil service block) which still stands today, close to the Jubilaumspark in Duisburg-Hamborn. A young widow, Brunhilde Bartling, lived nearby with her parents and other relatives in a four-storey block of flats at 7 Krienpoth Strasse. Brunhilde, often out walking, would watch with curiosity the guarded British parades in the area.

My father and Brunhilde would eventually meet each other in this park, despite instructions given to British troops to avoid German women. Brunhilde had been only fourteen years old when the war began. By then, Adolf Hitler had established firm control, following his early promises to lead Germany out of the huge economic slump of 1930-2.

In January 1933, the Nazi Party had persuaded the President of the Weimar Republic, Paul von Hindenburg, that Hitler should become Chancellor of the Reich. Although his party did not find a clear majority in the March election, Hitler arrested any members of the opposition parties who voted against him and subsequently abolished parliamentary government. His private army then systematically removed anyone who had publicly opposed him, while all other organisations, including religious organisations for children and young people, were either abolished or taken over by the Nazis. This suppression would impact seriously on many ordinary families such as Brunhilde's, with their strong Catholic upbringing and education.

Brunhilde was the second of five children in Bruno and Maria Bartling's family. Bruno was born in Harburg, Bavaria, in 1901 and Maria in Ottweiler, Saarland, in 1897. Bruno followed the Lutheran religion while Maria was a practising Catholic who insisted the children attend the local Catholic school opposite their home. Brunhilde loathed the Hitler Youth scheme which was promoted in school and regularly defied the imposed evening curfews, often cycling to and from friends' houses under darkness.

Until war broke out Bruno had worked nearby in Thyssen's steel mills, spending most of his spare time gardening in his allotment, where he grew fruit and vegetables. Maria remained at home looking after the family. Each year they reared a pig to make salamis, hams, and sausages; and kept geese, which not only provided eggs and meat, but feathers for the family's 'feather beds', or duvets as they are now known. The children were expected to help with various chores, including herding their geese and walking them to grazing ground across a nearby river bridge. This was a chore Brunhilde loathed, often commenting about the number of 'nips' they gave her on the journey!

After leaving school, Brunhilde, like her contemporaries, worked as part of the war effort, but again showed her determined nature by complaining about the poor food she was given when working on a farm in the south of the country. She was warned against complaining, in no uncertain terms, that repetition of this behaviour would most certainly send her off to a labour camp. Her real interest had been in dressmaking but her dream of becoming a seamstress was on hold.

In January 1944, Brunhilde married Hans Leibfried from

Saarbrücken in southern Germany in the small village of Hergisdorf in Saxony-Anhalt. In September that year, their son Hans Jurgen was born, but tragically, 24-year-old Hans Leibfried was killed the following year, just before the end of the war.

As the war continued, Brunhilde and her family were evacuated eastwards, away from the incessant bombing aimed at Germany's industrial Ruhr district. Between the 14th and 15th of October 1944, the allies dropped nearly 10,000 bombs on Duisburg. Whilst Brunhilde's family were away from their home, the neighbouring block of flats was completely sliced off by an Allied bomb; their upstairs elderly neighbour suffering a nervous breakdown as a result of the incessant bombing.

Eventually, the Bartling family returned to their home in Duisburg-Hamborn but life was increasingly hard. The German authorities had confiscated all the food available; Bruno's allotment had been ransacked and food was in desperately short supply. The family survived by making soup from anything that could be found, such as dandelions and grass. By the end of the war, Brunhilde's waistline was a mere eighteen inches.

In the Jubilaumspark one day, my father's attention was drawn to a very slim and attractive young German lady, despite the official warnings given to British soldiers about consorting with German women. The practice was seen as being dangerous and illegal, as many German women were described as being determined to marry British soldiers purely to get away from the bomb-ridden country. A handbook, *Instructions for British Servicemen in Germany, 1944* advised them that 'many German girls will be just waiting for the chance to marry a Briton' and that 'most of them will be infected!' Despite this warning, my father and Brunhilde began their romance and met each other regularly.

Given the circumstances of the time, it was inevitable that some would vehemently oppose their romance. Having noted the liaison between him and Brunhilde, serious attempts were made by others to put a stop to it. The treatment that followed was however inexcusable, especially given my father's bravery and devotion to

The Black Watch throughout his army career.

One example of this poor treatment was an accusation of criminal behaviour made against my father. He was accused of providing rations to Brunhilde's family and staying at their home. A Black Watch Company Sergeant Major named Johnson provided Brunhilde's address from headquarters to his commanding officer, Major Campbell, who ordered the Corps of Military Police (CMP – today known as the Royal Military Police) to search the house and particularly to look for 'Robert's bicycle'.

It is very clear from my father's letters to Lieutenant-Colonel Berrowald A. Innes, the Commanding Officer the 1st Battalion, The Black Watch, his statement of events, and a letter from a fellow soldier who also 'consorted with a German woman', that he was extremely disillusioned by and disgusted with the treatment he was receiving.

> To Lieutenant Colonel Berowald Alfred Innes.
> Sir,
>
> May I submit this letter to you for your judgement as to my best course of action in regard to the future. First, I would prefer a posting from where I am for the following reasons.
>
> I proceeded on leave on the 24th August and was told I could not have any money as there was none in the Company. This made it obvious that until I got money, I could not go to the rest camps until I was paid. Every day I was in barracks and my pass counterfoil was in HQ Company office so the question of suddenly wanting me did not make sense as I was probably in barracks at the time. It was obvious that there had been talk and that I was being checked on.
>
> When the CCG denied knowledge of me staying there surely that was sufficient without having to call in the CMPs to check on me and on top of all that for Major Campbell to order the CMPs to search my

German girl's house and were specially warned to look for my bicycle. To sum up the search – had I been found with one tin of sardines not on that day's ration or one-half pint of petrol then no power in the 1st Black Watch could have stopped proceedings.

Obviously, I have run foul of certain officers and having served my country and Regiment faithfully and taken some hard knocks in the war and come back for more, I think that such sadistic treatment as the above could make it safer for me to finish my time outside this Regiment in some employment where I may still make WO1 again.

It has not been very pleasant being posted to one of my Companies and my men seeing their RSM walking about as a CSM and I have still to do the same again if I am posted to the Depot. It all seems like either kicking a man when he is down or getting the last ounce of work out of an old horse.

Hoping that you will see my point and realise that my chances are better keeping away from the Regiment i.e. while the army is still at peace.

Sir

Signed R. Roy CSM A Company the 1st Battalion, The Black Watch

My father detailed the events at that time.

Before I went on leave the Col was asked could I have it during the period that the Battalion was at camp. The answer was that the CO would prefer me to go to camp and have leave after.

A few days before the Battalion left for camp the Adjutant informed me that the CO now wanted me to have leave when the Battalion was at camp.

The Adjutant being a gentleman implored on me to

go home to the UK and not take a leave locally. This request was repeated about three times which I put down to the Adjutant thinking that I had been too long without a leave, which was over a year.

Although OC HQ knew in plenty of time that I was going on leave I was informed on the day I was due to go that he was sorry that there was no money in the Coy and would I mind waiting a few days. This was on a Saturday.

Had I been paid on the Saturday I would have been on my way to Monasee [Möhnesee] rest camp. Every day I was in the camp and in the Mess at night. My rations were collected daily from the Mess which was in order with Rhine Army standing orders that anyone visiting German families could take their food.

I had made sure that the messing Sergeant was informed that I was not claiming ration money and would collect rations for the daily period that I was not messing in barracks.

As I pointed out in para 6, I was in camp every day. Yet I was wanted and had to be found through my address on my pass. I reported to the orderly room and received the unintelligent reply from the person who was checking up on me that he did not want me, but Major Campbell did.

As I had reported too promptly nothing could be said re my address so the CMPs were then sent to 628 Mil Gov to check up if I lived there. The CMPs reported that I was not living at 628 but could not prove that I had lived other than in barracks.

A new angle was tried. That was rations – which has been explained. This could not be proved. The most damning move of all – the CMPs were ordered to search my girl's house where a pair of spare laces would have been sufficient to condemn me.

To sum up, I was meant to be held in the Duisburg area for at least two days with no money so as to be tempted to be found sleeping in a German house. As one thing cleared another – more methods were tried with sadistic tendencies to trap me at all costs. Had I been stationed in the UK and on leave, then it would have been sufficient if my address was phoned and I was able to be informed and report accordingly. That the whole thing was arranged and was known to more than two officers borne out by the fact that was told later that an officer was heard to state, "I'll get that. . . yet" and the Adjutant being so insistent that I go to UK which is the only clean thing in this episode.

I cannot understand why I was not allowed to wait the other month and a half to pull my subs, x rank and then posted as a WO1 extra Reg Empl. and not ridiculed as I was by being posted to one of my own Companies for about 6 weeks and then to the Regimental Depot as a WO2.

A letter to my father from another soldier, I. Burch, of Lincolnshire, who married a German, described similar treatment. His full kit, packed up and ready for him to leave for Duisburg was stolen the day before travel, leaving him to remain for three weeks for a court of inquiry. On arrival in Duisburg he was told that his three months DV had ended and he had to leave for demobilisation the following morning. This was three days before he had arranged to get married. He then signed on for another six months as he knew it would take two or three weeks to receive a reply from 2 No ECH. He was given one day off to get married then sent off on escort for four days, before another dispatch for a week. With no further escort duties to be carried out he reported to the Regimental Sergeant Major.

•

Who delivered the message from the CO that I was to take down my third stripe and return to C Company drafting Company. I was only back at C Company for four days when I was called for at the BOR and was told that my six months had been refused. I was also told unofficially that my papers got no farther than the CO's office.

The next problem was that I was due to be sent on release and the papers for my wife's passport were not in. The next two days I knew everyone was looking for me to warn me for release the following day. No-one had the sense to put this on detail. Those two days I went to Dusseldorf and all over the place and finally got everything complete. I was warned for release at 5 o'clock at night; by 7 o'clock everything was handed in and I went to spend my last night down home with the wife.

She cooked me a good meal and we opened two bottles of stuff we had been saving for Christmas, but it seems they were still out to get me even to the last because at 12 o'clock that night there was a knock at the door – it was Sergeant Hird and one RP. They said there had been some blankets taken from 77 British Hospital and they hoped I would not mind if they had a look around. So, they searched the house from top to bottom and did not find a thing. That of course, was just an excuse to search the house.

The next morning, I was away on the demob truck and I can tell you I was glad to get away from 1st Black Watch. PS I almost forgot – you may already know this, but I found out that the man that fetched Hilda's (Brunhilde's) address from HQ Company office when you were on leave was Command Sergeant Major Johnson. I can let you have the particulars if you want them.

This disgraceful episode affected my father considerably. Proud of his confidential reports that highlighted him as 'a fine Regimental soldier who always has the best interests of his Regiment at heart' and as 'outstanding in intelligence, initiative and zeal', he had found it abhorrent to then experience such underhand treatment by some in his own regiment after 26 years' loyal service.

CHAPTER 7

SCOTLAND

FORTUNATELY, my father had true friends in The Black Watch. He was posted back to Britain in September 1947 with Warrant Officer Class 1 Regimental Sergeant Major status and was obviously a much happier man back with his regiment in Perth, carrying out his usual duties, including military parades in the area.

He went to stay briefly with his sister Jane (Jean) Owens, whose husband Frank had retrieved his pipes from the Grafacos family in Athens. On 16th October, he wrote to Hilda:

> My darling Hilda I have arrived in Scotland safely and at the moment am having a few days' leave with my sister before starting work as a soldier again. It is going to be much better as the old officers are all men who have been good soldiers in the war and I always find that type make good officers in peace.
>
> I have applied for papers to marry you – so you will be with me early next year. My sister and my aunt are both happy to hear that I am marrying you. My aunt, who is the drum major's mother (Mary Roy) is going to give you a room in her house until I can get a house of our own...
>
> Sgt Burch and his wife Heney will, if they can manage, be our best man and best maid and I will ask George Punter and Monica and all the old friends to try and come to our wedding... Sergeant Burch is in Glasgow just now and is with me every day.
>
> I will send you some food as soon as possible...

•

On 28th October that year, he was presented with the DCM by King George VI at Buckingham Palace.

By November, my father wrote to Duisburg to let Hilda know that he was enjoying his new post as Company Sergeant, 42 Primary Training Centre in A Company, Perth. During this period, he continued to organise and instruct the pipe band, being honoured to play before Field Marshal Archibald Wavell and the Queen (mother).

My father had already saved money and clothing coupons for Hilda. However, he explained in his letter to her:

> The papers are taking a long time to come from Berlin, so I am going to write again tonight (12 November) although I think you will have them long before Christmas.

Again, he promised to send coffee, food, and chocolate to her, understanding how difficult it was for the German family. He also asked Hilda to photograph his dog Ralph, whom he intended to bring back to Scotland later.

Unfortunately, my father's optimism in seeing Hilda before Christmas was not confirmed and the two were still apart. On 13th February 1948, he wrote to Martin Bencher Ltd (shipping, forwarding, and insurance agents in London) with the questions:

> Could I have more details in regard to the following:
> I am intending marrying a German girl and have received word from the Foreign Office that an exit permit and a visa have been issued to my fiancé to travel to the UK. It has been pointed out in the letter that I can have her brought over here either by official or private means. The official means is liable to take at least a month and probably more.
> Can you please tell me the approximate waiting period on a passage by air through your agency? The full charge and information required.

If your arrangements suit me, will it be sufficient if I wire you to carry on? I would like particulars of the scheme regarding furniture of German nationals being imported. As this case has been a long drawn out affair, I hope you will treat the reply as urgent. I cannot reply to the Foreign Office until I have your answer.

The 'long drawn out affair' continued and by 2nd March, Martin Bencher advised my father:

We have no news yet – other than information from Hamburg that they were contacting the lady. Experience has shown that passengers do not reply to the offer of accommodation made. We suggest that you telegraph the lady, telling her to get in touch with: Messrs. British European Airways, Hapag Building, Ballingdamm 25, Hamburg saying fare paid through Martin Bencher Ltd, voucher 21/2, when she can travel.

At long last, Hilda arrived in Scotland where she (aged 22) and my father (aged 38) married in Perth, at West Church Manse, Brompton Terrace, on 30th March 1948, with Sergeant Burch and his wife Heney as their best man and best maid.

———————

CHAPTER 8

POST-WAR

MY FATHER was by now seriously searching for civilian accommodation, knowing that his regular army service was coming to its end, though he still continued in the TA. As a career soldier, he knew little about housing applications and waiting lists, but optimistically wrote an application to Glasgow Corporation in June 1948 detailing his many years of army service. Almost one month later, The Corporation of Glasgow sent him a postcard stating 'that, owing to the excessive number of applicants entitled to prior consideration, it is not possible to deal with your case meantime. Your application will be given consideration in due course'.

Fortunately, my father was posted as Company Sergeant Major to Kirkcaldy's TA Centre in Hunter Street shortly afterwards and began his married life in an army flat in David Street, Kirkcaldy, where I was born on 6th January 1949.

During this time, several regimental colleagues' weddings took place, and my father and his bagpipes were in demand. On 19th February, he played at the wedding of The Black Watch officer Henry Butler McKenzie Johnstone and Mariam Allardyce Middleton at St Giles Cathedral, Edinburgh. Johnstone had been with 6th Battalion in Tunisia, Italy, and Greece.

My father continued to be concerned about housing for the family and in April he wrote to Kirkcaldy town factor J. Lees.

> May I submit this application for consideration by the housing committee.
>
> I will have 21 pensionable years' service on 15th July this year. I occupy an army house which is on the same principle as a single soldier and on changing jobs or finishing I am required to vacate this house the same

day as I finish. As we have a baby three months old this is not very heartening.

I intend to settle in Kirkcaldy and will probably continue to help out with the TA movement.

As will be seen on the attached war record, I have been on active service from 1937 till 1947 and had not the faintest idea where to settle till being posted home on October 1947. I trust that will explain why my application has not been applied for before 1948.

Fortuitously, new housing was being built rapidly in the town and my parents were allocated the newly built three-bedroom property at 81 Winifred Crescent, where my sister Margaret was born in June 1950.

My father enjoyed his posting in Hunter Street TA Centre and continued to instruct novice pipers. He befriended and tutored a young piper, Jim Anderson from Methil, often bringing him to the family home for meals. The accomplished piper William Brown from Kelty received his first 'Piobaireachd' instruction from my father that same year.

On the 15th November 1950, Bernard Fergusson wrote to my father from White's, St James's Street, London SW1A saying:

> Dear Roy,
> It is nearly 20 years since you were my platoon piper and I am delighted that you are able and willing to play me over the top. Captain Atkins has all instructions for you and I look forward to seeing you. With you playing, I know that I shall be properly married!

On 22nd November that year, Bernard Fergusson married Laura Margaret Grenfell, daughter of Lieutenant-Colonel Arthur Morton Grenfell, with my father duly in attendance to once again play the pipes for his good friend. Fergusson sent a note of thanks to 'My dear Pipe Major and old friend'.

Around this time, my father was considering his future career. Friends and former colleagues suggested various options, including working at Queen Victoria School, Dunblane, as Piping Instructor, or in Australia, emigration to South Africa, or working for former officers on their Highland estates. One particular friend from the 2nd Battalion, Professor A. Berry, wrote between 1949 and 1951 urging my father to visit him at his ranch in Rhodesia to have a look, saying, 'this country would suit you'.

Berry had last seen my father in India, and after leaving Germany in 1946 when he was Officer Commanding HQ Company, the 2nd Battalion, he had married a doctor in the Royal Army Medical Corps, before they had both moved to South Africa. By 1949, they were running Lendy Ranch, Marandella, and had two young sons. Amusingly, he described his sons' possible futures:

> If they grow up with any brains, we'll not know what to do with them. If they don't, it will be just too easy: send them to Sandhurst!

In his 1951 letter, Berry alluded to some of their past service, and to the number of former battalion soldiers who had settled in South Africa, still trying to persuade my father to move there too.

> Last year when the 1st Battalion came to Rhodesia I had Hirko and some of the band out here, including Pipe Sgt Irvine. They seemed to enjoy it. I laid on a shoot for them and we had the beaters out. But although plenty of deer were flushed out no one managed to hit anything despite their blazing away about a hundred rounds. I don't think they can be getting enough shooting practice in the Battalion!
>
> There are quite a few old BW out here, but the one I least expected to see was Snub McKinlay. Jack Noble is another old 2nd Battalion man out here. He's a Captain in the RAR. When I left the 2nd Battalion

there were only two of us in it left who came with us from the Middle East. The colonel John Benson and myself and a couple of days before I left Tony McGibbon came back.

It seems a long time since we parted company in Ranchi and since we visited that Doctor bloke and his coloured wife in Contai village. I wonder if you still remember going to his house? I don't suppose you will ever forget how you caught up with Private Ross after he got away with the PRI cash!

Another old 2nd Battalion man out here permanently is Major Richard Flemming. He is farming near Salisbury.

My father wrote to Professor Berry on 24th November 1951 recalling:

[The] happy days among men who could be rough and joke and face death with the same smile. Your Rhodesian platoon fitted in with the battalion to a man and more than upheld the traditions of The Black Watch.

Revealingly, he also informed Professor Berry that after leaving the 2nd Battalion, he went over to France with the Highland Division in the 7th Battalion.

[And] although they were very reasonable, they never quite came up to the 2nd. I married a very nice German girl which of course was frowned upon by some of the powers that be, who noticeably had seen very little of the Germans in the field. This was the type who I found hated the Germans most; not the men who had fought them.

The family stayed in Scotland.

In 1952, Bernard Fergusson, by then Colonel of the Regiment, arranged for my father, along with piper, Lance Corporal Grieve, to attend the Paris headquarters of General Eisenhower at SHAPE (Supreme Headquarters Allied Powers Europe). General Eisenhower was due for retirement and it was well known then that he would be a candidate for the forthcoming American presidential election. They dined with the colonel and his wife and then travelled on to the reception where Eisenhower gave a speech of honour to the two pipers, outlining their outstanding war records. Bernard Fergusson later wrote:

> In 1951, when I was serving at SHAPE, I caused him (Robert) to be flown over in an RAF aircraft to play before General Eisenhower and 400 officers of 12 different nations at dinner. The RAF pilot confided to me that while they were over the English Channel, he had induced Roy to put a tune on the pipes and had relayed it for a full minute over his transmitter, to the certain astonishment of all other aircraft on the frequency. I had prepared a note for General Eisenhower concerning Roy's record and history, which he read out in full in Roy's presence (standing stiffly to attention) to all the company. Later I heard Eisenhower start a conversation with him on the subject of 'Pipers I have known'. Roy listened politely and then embarked on 'American Generals I have known'.

My father and piper Grieve were then both presented with a personally autographed photograph of both men and General Eisenhower. On their return, my father was interviewed by a local reporter and told him he was impressed with General Eisenhower, who was obviously greatly loved by his own men and British soldiers alike. He also added, 'Relations among all other ranks and officers, particularly between Americans and British, were extremely good'.

Shortly afterwards, my father was offered another posting to Dundee. With permission to sub-let Winifred Crescent until his return to Kirkcaldy, a town which he liked very much, the family moved to stay firstly in the drill hall flat in Bell Street, Dundee, next to the police station, where a strong friendship existed between the military and the police.

One test of this friendship occurred one day when my sister Margaret and I decided to free canaries from our father's prized aviary. Margaret opened the door and, waving a stick, chased the birds out. Minutes later, the police neighbours were seen chasing across Dundee on a rescue mission!

My father continued to teach the pipes in the drill hall to his recruits and also to the caretaker's young daughter Anne, whose youth had been blighted by Polio. He treated her as one of his own daughters, giving her a set of bagpipes and teaching her to read music.

From Bell Street, the family moved to Old Craigie Road, by then acquiring Ralph, an Alsatian puppy, and soon afterwards to Dennison Road opposite the army camp. My sister and I started school at Glebelands Primary, a short walk away through Baxter Park. My mother then took a position at Dundee's Timex factory, dealing with the mail and generally life took on a pleasant routine.

On the evenings when my father instructed beginner pipers, mother would disappear to the 'pictures', seeking some respite from the many different tunes (and attempts at tunes) being played in every room of the bungalow. My sister and I, left to our own devices, played around the house, and listened in to some of the tunes. On one particular evening we decorated the hall wall with crayons – discovered only by mother on her return – but instead of hearing the worst, heard my father say, 'Aren't they clever to write all this!'

One final letter was sent to Glasgow Corporation in 1953, explaining that my father now had a family of two daughters. My father was still considering moving back to his home city and relatives there, but yet again was unsuccessful, despite waiting to be housed there for five years. That same year came the shocking news of his brother Neil's death of a cerebral haemorrhage on 6th August at the untimely age of only 30 years. (Neil had completed his army service and was then working as a general labourer in Swansea.)

CHAPTER 9

THE MBE AND GIBRALTAR

IN JUNE 1956, my father was awarded an MBE by Her Majesty Queen Elizabeth at Buckingham Palace. We accompanied a very proud soldier to the Palace to watch him being decorated by the Queen. Congratulatory telegrams and letters followed from various parts of the world.

From Dundee, came three telegrams, from Regimental Sergeant Major, Warrant Officers, and Sergeants, the 1st Battalion, The Black Watch: 'Heartiest congratulations on your recent award'. From Ex-Company Sergeant Henderson C Company congratulating the Regimental Sergeant Major: 'with best wishes for the future'. A third from Company Quartermaster Sergeant J. K.

On 1st June a letter arrived from Bernard Fergusson.

> My dear Roy,
>
> Nothing that has happened for a long time has given me such pleasure as your MBE, and hundreds of other people will be rejoicing with me. I am really delighted, and no honour was ever more deserved. My wife joins with me in offering her warmest and heartiest congratulations.
>
> Your old friend
> Bernard Fergusson

In a similar manner, on the same date, Major General Neil McMicking, Colonel of The Black Watch wrote:

> My dear RSM Roy
> My many congratulations on your MBE which I was delighted to hear about.

I think you and Colonel Brodie are our only recipients this time. He has just gone off to Laos from Korea. I expect he'll be off behind the Iron Curtain next!

Best wishes and congratulations again.

Neil McMicking

On 5th June, W. R. R. Bruce wrote supportively from Broughty Ferry.

Dear RSM

It was with great pleasure that I read of your honour in the Birthday list. I can assure you that you have certainly deserved it, and may you have many more years in The Black Watch to enjoy it.

W. Bruce

On 15th June, Major J. C. Monteith wrote a note of congratulations from British Forces Post Office 45 (Berlin).

Dear RSM

Many congratulations on your MBE, which I was delighted to see in the Birthday Honours.

The belts arrived safely while I was on leave – many thanks for them and for your note.

The Pipes and Drums are coming along very well, and we can now put over twenty pipers on parade again, although this three-year engagement makes it a constant struggle.

They have made a very good impression here and are much in demand. At present they are in Paris on a three-day engagement in connection with the Liberation Anniversary Celebrations. They will be home for the Edinburgh Tattoo and there will probably be two very interesting tours coming off, one this Autumn and the other next spring.

> If you have any young entry coming along, please
> send us a copy of anything you send to the Depot. I was
> upset to find Piper Simpson had been trained as a clerk
> instead of a piper. He is now with the Pipes and Drums
> in Paris, but it took months to straighten things out!

Between 23rd July and 4th August 1956, my father carried out
the somewhat unusual task of performing at Dundee Repertory
Theatre in Rosamunde Pilcher's play *The Piper of Orde*.

In 1956, the family returned to Kirkcaldy for a short time
together, before my father was posted later the following year to
Gibraltar as Garrison Sergeant Major.

In February 1957, Earle Nicoll, one of my father's wartime
colleagues from the early days in India and by then a colonel, wrote
to request his presence as piper at his wedding in March at St John's
Church, Banbury. He said he was delighted to hear from Captain
Arbuthnott that my father had agreed and told him that Colonel
David Rose would be attending. He wrote:

> I am thrilled that you're to be there. So will my father
> be who seems to bump into everyone now and again in
> Dundee. PS I haven't congratulated you yet on your
> MBE. Very good effort and well deserved!

Not long afterwards, we travelled to join my father in Gibraltar,
on the troopship Dunera, particularly enjoying the rough swells of the
Bay of Biscay and watching the deckchairs as they slid from side to side.

Our family lived in the Garrison Sergeant Major's house, mid-way
up the 'Rock', complete with roof water tank, outhouses, and walled
garden (which were unusual on Gibraltar). School was operated
from a classroom in the barracks, run by a retired colonel's daughter,
with lessons being taught between 8 am and 1 pm.

Once more, a pleasant routine developed. Most afternoons we
went to Catalan Bay beach with friends, taking the bus that drove
through the tunnels to the shore. We frequently walked to the top of

the 'Rock' to see the apes who loved to rifle through pockets and tear off any available windscreen wipers and to visit St Michael's Cave. Geraniums grew wild on the 'Rock' and much to the neighbouring Gibraltarian families' mirth, my parents planted some of these in the garden. We acquired a kitten and rabbits and it was not unusual to find the kitten asleep with them in the hutch under the orange tree.

In those days, water was brought round in large buckets to the local families who lined up to fill their containers. Rainwater was collected in large troughs on the 'Rock' but was often in short supply. No cows existed, apart from one owned by the Governor, so milk was brought to Gibraltar in frozen bags. The border to Spain was open but guarded and many confiscated cars were to be seen in no-man's land.

We had a Spanish maid, Angela, who travelled daily from and to La Linea to look after our house. However, although mother welcomed her help, she was determined to do her own laundry, much to Angela's surprise. We soon learned that mother had a fastidious approach to laundry that would never change during her lifetime.

My father continued to promote piping on the 'Rock' and also became very involved in instructing the 5th Gibraltar Sea Scouts Pipe Band.

Before his departure, the Gibraltar Sea Scouts presented him with a photograph showing him in their midst and inscribed:

To Mr R. Roy, with kindest appreciation
from the 5th Group, Gibraltar (Sea Scouts) Band.
M. Hernandez,
Group Scoutmaster
14/6/60

•

My father was also welcomed to many events shared by the British and American navies whose ships berthed in Gibraltar. In February 1958, my parents were presented with several photographs of the US Marines and United States Navy.

The pleasant family stay in Gibraltar came to an abrupt end, when President Nasser of Egypt declared he would nationalise the Suez Canal, contrary to the 1888 Treaty. Anthony Eden, Hugh Gaitskell, and other world leaders viewed this action as requiring urgent action to prevent its loss as a major shipping route. Consequently, it was decided to return all military wives and children to the UK as a safety precaution, though in the end the problem was resolved without any military action. So, once again, the family was separated for a time, with father remaining in Gibraltar to finish his tour.

In September 1959, while my father was still in Gibraltar and the rest of us in Kirkcaldy, my brother Robert was born at 81 Winifred Crescent. My father returned the following early spring, by this time now seriously trying to decide where his future lay. In the spring of 1960 my father was appointed Garrison Sergeant Major at Edinburgh Castle. As this would most likely be his final appointment given his age, he and my mother discussed various options and it seemed likely that he would accept an invitation to move to Australia to lead a piping school there. The suggestion of working on a Highland estate had not gone down well with mother.

Meantime, the eleven-plus exam loomed for me, and realising I had some weaknesses in arithmetic, my father collected text books from his friend Ronnie Wood, the headmaster at Valley Primary School and spent many evenings tutoring me. He also worked vigorously in the large garden, which had been too big for us to maintain well while he had been away. A spot of painting followed, though mother vowed never to let him do this chore again when she saw the 'completed' bathroom. My father had quite correctly decided to cover the bath to prevent paint dripping into it but had stuck the protective paper to the bath rim with paint.

Around this time, a young boy named Peter Snaddon, who lived nearby in Hendry Crescent, would often watch my father as he walked to Hunter Street TA centre. Peter later became a renowned piper with The Black Watch and has said he was inspired by my father to follow this career.

———————

PHOTOGRAPH
SECTION

2

TOBRUK, GERMANY, SCOTLAND, AND GIBRALTAR

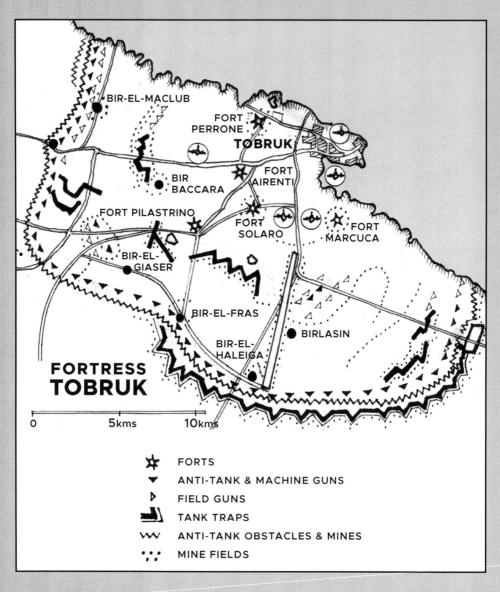

BIR-EL-MACLUB

FORT PERRONE

TOBRUK

BIR BACCARA

FORT AIRENTI

FORT PILASTRINO

FORT SOLARO

FORT MARCUCA

BIR-EL-GIASER

BIR-EL-FRAS

BIRLASIN

BIR-EL-HALEIGA

FORTRESS TOBRUK

0   5kms   10kms

✵ FORTS

▼ ANTI-TANK & MACHINE GUNS

▷ FIELD GUNS

TANK TRAPS

Ⓥ ANTI-TANK OBSTACLES & MINES

MINE FIELDS

20—Map of the Battle for the Relief of the Tobruk Garrison, November 1941.

BRITISH AND NEW ZEALAND COMMANDERS MEET IN THE TOBRUK CORRIDOR.

SUNSET OVER THE DESERT, AND SMILES ON THE FACES OF INFANTRY UNITS WHO HAVE COME TO GREET THE CREWS OF BRITISH TANKS FROM TOBRUK WHICH FIRST SALLIED OUT TO JOIN UP WITH THE IMPERIAL FORCES OF GENERAL AUCHINLECK'S EIGHTH ARMY

21—'Sunset over the desert, and smiles on the faces of infantry units who have come to greet the crews of British tanks from Tobruk which first sallied out to join the Imperial Forces of General Auchinleck's Eighth Army'. *Illustrated London News,* 20th December 1941.

THE CAIRN
15 miles South East of TOBRUK

21 Nov. 1941.   11 Jan. 1942.

22—The Cairn, fifteen miles south east of Tobruk.

23—Robert Roy on leave in Glasgow, after the relief of the
Tobruk Garrison and before Germany.

24—Robert Roy in Germany – on left.

25—Robert Roy in Germany – on right.

26—Robert Roy in Germany, outside barracks – centre.

27—Robert Roy and Hilda in Germany.

28—Wedding of Robert Roy and Hilda, Perth, 30th March 1948.

29—Trafalgar Square on day of Robert Roy's MBE Award at Buckingham Palace, 31st May 1956. Left to right: Margaret, Hilda, and Alice.

30—Marriage of Brigadier Bernard Fergusson to Laura Margaret Grenfell,
22nd November 1950 .

31—Robert Roy as Gibraltar Garrison Sergeant Major.

32—Left to right: Lance Corporal J. Grieve, General Eisenhower, and Pipe Major Robert Roy.

33—5th Group Gibraltar Sea Scouts Band, 14th June 1960.

CHAPTER 10

EPILOGUE

IN 1960, as Garrison Sergeant Major, my father was asked to be the 'Lone Piper' at that year's Edinburgh Tattoo. He stayed in the castle for rehearsals the week before the event, (also the week when I learned I had passed the eleven-plus exam), but died suddenly during the night on 24th August, aged 51. Like his grandmother and his brother Neil before him, the cause of death was a brain haemorrhage.

Many letters of condolence were sent to my mother, now at the young age of 35, a widow again, with three young children, including eleven-month old Robert. Neighbours and friends rallied round, though naturally all were distraught. Headmaster Ronnie Wood at Valley Primary called my sister and I into his office to give us the sad news, showing his truly compassionate nature. My class teacher, Ian Finlayson, newly qualified after his period in the RAF, was also very supportive and kind to us.

Mother's best friend Inge, also German by birth and the wife of local miner and former Black Watch soldier Ernest Hogg, stayed by her side to offer support and help with the family.

Letters of sympathy arrived from both officers and men of the Regiment.

David Arbuthnott (Warminster):
What a help he was to me during our time together in Dundee.

John Morrow (Cowglen Military Hospital):
Mr Roy was not only well known in the army but well-loved. He was not only a very loyal and courageous soldier but also a very kind and understanding warrant officer, as those who have

had the honour and pleasure to serve under him can testify. His example and devotion to duty will long be remembered not only by his own very famous regiment The Black Watch, but also by those of the other arms of the service who were fortunate enough to know him.

Lieutenant G. Paterson, The Black Watch (Nottingham):
Your husband was a good friend of mine and I admired him tremendously. He was a fine soldier and will be sadly missed by all who knew him.

Captain Gordon (Queen's Barracks, Perth):
The grief which we all feel at the passing of your husband cannot possibly be as great as yours. All of us at the Depot will miss the RSM very much indeed. Your husband was not only a great man on the battlefield but a kind soldier who gave a tremendous amount to The Black Watch and to the British Army. He was a great teacher of young pipers...

Lieutenant-Colonel Ronald Skeates, OBE
(Royal Army Pay Corps):
We were all proud to have your husband here with us in Edinburgh Castle and were looking forward to his being with us for some time to come. On behalf of all ranks in the Castle, I offer our deepest sympathy and that you will be comforted by the knowledge of your husband's wonderful service record, which has been such an inspiration to us all.

Warrant Officer 2 Adcock
(Garrison Sergeants' Mess, Gibraltar):
While it has not been my pleasure to meet you and your family, I have spent many a happy hour

discussing life in general with Rob. There is no doubt your husband was devoted mainly to the service and I and every other member of the mess sincerely regret your sad loss.

The Reverend Peter MacEwen
(St Andrew's Church, Gibraltar):
It seems such a short time since we were saying goodbye to him on the Rock, confident that sometime and some place we would meet again. However, it is not to be, but I shall always be glad that I was privileged to know him for our first three years on the Rock: and how we shall miss the gallant, jaunty figure swinging across Governor's Parade, his eyes alert and missing nothing, but with a greeting for all he knew – and there seemed few people for whom he did not have a word in the morning.

How magnificent he was in all the glory of his full-dress uniform when he would 'gie us a blaw' on the pipes. In himself there seemed to be so much of what was toughest and best in his great regiment and in the Highland Division where his name will never be forgotten...

Major Hitchman (Queen's Barracks, Perth):
We shall always treasure the memory of his brave and active life with the Regiment and the many kindnesses he showed to his fellow comrades when called upon for advice or help...

Lieutenant-Colonel McLeod (15 The Links, St Andrews):
You will not know me, but I was your late husband's commanding officer in Glasgow in about 1937 and it was I that promoted him to the Pipe Major of the 2nd Battalion. I have since followed his progress with

*interest and especially his gallant action at Tobruk. I
had left the Regiment of course by then. My wife and I
were interested when we saw that he had gone to
Gibraltar as Garrison Sergeant Major, one of his latest
appointments. My wife and I spent nearly four years
on the Rock when I was on the Staff then in 1924-27.*

Condolences came from many people, including **Henry** and
Joan Burch (Lincolnshire), **Major Seath** (Kirkcaldy), **Mr and
Mrs Lees** (he the Kirkcaldy town factor), **Ronald Wood**
(Headteacher of Valley Primary School, Kirkcaldy), and countless
neighbours and friends across the country.

Two particularly poignant letters came from people mother had
never known.

Mrs Davidson (Cardenden):

*You will not know me, and I only met your husband
once – that was the day of my father's funeral back
in 1951. My father had a military funeral and your
husband played his Tobruk pipes in the funeral
march. I felt so proud as my father was an old Black
Watch man himself…*

The second was from **Peter Moran** (Perth):

*I was deeply in sorrow to have read about the death
of your husband as we were both brought up in the
same place (Camlachie in Glasgow) and were at the
same school. Many's a happy day his family and our
own had spent together in our young days. The first
time I met Robert after many years was at a camp
outside Scarborough and after that I met him here
in Perth Black Watch barracks. I am terribly sorry
to hear such news about an old friend…*

•

With the help of Lieutenant-Colonel Ronald Skeates at Edinburgh Castle, preparations began for my father's funeral with full military honours. The service was conducted by the Reverend John Simpson, Minister of St John's Church (Elgin Street, Kirkcaldy).

Crowds lined the street outside Hayfield Cemetery as the cortege arrived and the bearers moved slowly to the graveside behind the young piper Jim Anderson, whom my father had taught to play years earlier. About 400 mourners stood silent in the sunshine; the bugler sounded the *Last Post*, rifles fired three times, and once more the pipes were heard in the lament *Lochaber No More*.

Amongst those mourning at the cemetery that day were those with whom Robert had served in his long military career. These included General R. K. Arbuthnott, Colonel of the Regiment, Major General Neil McMicking, a former Colonel of the Regiment. Both men had been commanding officers in Palestine and Egypt, with the latter being commander of the 2nd Battalion during the Palestine emergency of 1938-9. Bernard Fergusson, Robert's first platoon commander was another mourner with a strong connection to my father. Fergusson had appointed my father as his own piper back in the early 1930s when both were young soldiers. Among the many other mourners were Colonel G. W. Dunn (TA Arbroath), Colonel C. N. Thomson (TA Dundee), Lieutenant-Colonel Ronald Skeates (Edinburgh Castle), Major General F. C. C. Graham (Perth), and Major (Doctor) Petrie of David Street, Kirkcaldy who was closely connected with my father through the TA and as his neighbour in David Street, Kirkcaldy, in 1948.

Numerous other members of the Regiment came from far and wide to bid farewell to their highly-respected colleague and friend. Among the 400 mourners present were those who knew the 'Piper of Tobruk' as a quiet family man in Kirkcaldy, who always had a kind word for everyone who knew him.

The mourners stood silent and many wept in the melancholy air, bidding farewell to a hero and friend and signalling the end of an amazing, frequently dangerous, and adventurous life that began from humble origins.

My father was buried in a grave that sits at almost the furthest point of the main path into Hayfield Cemetery, a peaceful spot originally beneath an old oak tree.

Newspaper headlines the week of the funeral announced:

'Last lament for 'Piper of Tobruk'
'Generals and humble privates join in Tribute'
'A Lament for Rob Roy on his own Pipes'

Bernard Fergusson wrote the obituary in the *Red Hackle*:

Regimental Sergeant Major Robert Roy, who died suddenly on the 24th August 1960 in Edinburgh, where he had just been appointed Garrison Sergeant Major, was beyond question the most famous 'Jock' of his generation, of whatever regiment and will certainly always be remembered in the history of my own. He joined The Black Watch in 1926 at the age of 18, coming of an old regimental family. As our history tells us, it was a private Duncan Roy of the 42nd who spread his blanket over Sir Ralph Abercrombie when he was fatally wounded at the Battle of Aboukir in 1801; and although there is no certainty that this was a direct forebear, Roy was at least the fourth generation to serve in the Regiment.

I find it impossible to write of him with detachment, since I knew him at the very beginning of my service. In 1931, every platoon had its own piper and I inherited Roy as mine; the NCOs were Sergeant Wilkinson, Corporal (now Major) Jim Ewen, Corporal Jack (killed in Palestine before the war), Lance Corporal 'Snapper' Lawrence and Lance Corporal 'Boy' McKinlay, who was to win the Military Cross as a CSM in the break-out from Tobruk. Changes were less frequent in those days and this team hung together for a couple of years. Roy, then twenty-three, was already the mixture of stolidity and romance that became such a familiar figure later on. He was already a good piper and player of 'Piobaireachd', with a large repertoire, and was inexhaustible on the longest of marches. He had in his possession a platoon group photograph of those days, shewing him standing solemnly at the end of the back row with his pipes.

Sir Bernard then continued with a description of the events in Crete and Tobruk, adding:

His exploits are part of the fabric of our history and need not be told afresh. It is an open secret that he was recommended for the Victoria Cross.

For some years after the war he was RSM of the 1st Battalion in Germany and subsequently of the 4/5th. Thence in 1957 he went to Gibraltar as Garrison Sergeant Major, from which appointment he returned only a few weeks before his sudden death. Early in December 1958 I was visiting Rabat, the capital of Morocco and found that I had missed by only a couple of days his playing at a dinner in the British Embassy on St Andrew's Night; he had left for me a long recording on tape of all the tunes I used to badger him to play when I was his platoon commander 27 years before...

As a devoted son of the Regiment, in every respect, he was unsurpassed. His devotion to it was blind and he gave it all he had, body and soul. Except for his family, he had literally no interest in the world except for the music of the pipes and the regiment of his birth. He certainly relished the soubriquet 'The Piper of Tobruk', which the press bestowed upon him; but he regarded it chiefly as a Battle Honour which he personally had been able to win for the Regiment. It is given to few, to do as much. He was a grand man.

PHOTOGRAPH
SECTION

3

PIPE MAJOR ROBERT ROY –
BALHOUSIE CASTLE,
REGIMENTAL MUSEUM OF THE
BLACK WATCH, PERTH – HOLDINGS

34—Balhousie Castle, Regimental Museum of The Black Watch, Perth.

35—Blue bonnet hackle belonging to
Regimental Sergeant Major Robert Roy.
(2012.94.9 – in store)

36—Brown leather piper's cross belt belonging to Pipe Major Robert Roy. (2012.94.4 – in store)

37—Green Jacket, 'No. 1 Dress', with three rows of Medal Ribbons plus 'Mention in Dispatches', eighteen buttons, 'Warrant Officer Class 1' badge on sleeve belonging to Regimental Sergeant Major Robert Roy. (A2698 – in store)

38—Green khaki jacket, with full length sleeves with turned up cuffs and Lion Decoration on sleeve, shoulder straps fastened with silver Black Watch buttons, left and right waist and breast pockets with flap, fastened with four buttons, ribbons above left breast pocket [enlargement inset]: War Defence Medal; British Empire, Imperial Service Order; General Service Medal 1918-62, 1939-45 Star, Africa Star; Burma Star, France Germany Star, Defence Medal, Second World War Medal with Oak Leaf pin; Army LS & GC Second Type, Second World War Service Medal, belonging to Regimental Sergeant Major Robert Roy. (2012.94.2 - in store)

40—Photograph of Pipe Major Robert Roy, 1942-3.
(A3796 – in store)

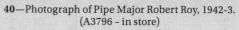

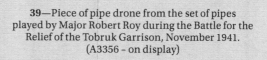

39—Piece of pipe drone from the set of pipes
played by Major Robert Roy during the Battle for the
Relief of the Tobruk Garrison, November 1941.
(A3356 – on display)

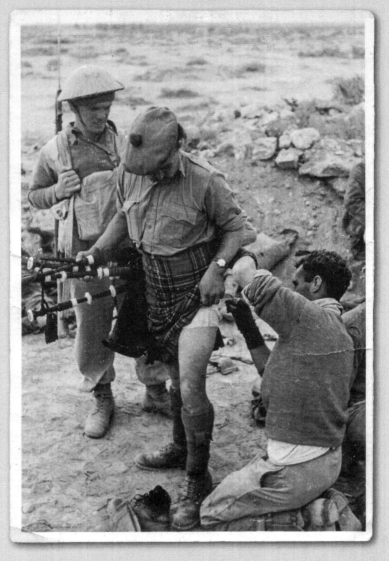

41—Photograph of Pipe Major Robert Roy being treated for one of his wounds received during the Battle for the Relief of the Tobruk Garrison, November, 1941. (A5312.2 – on display)

42—Royal Stewart tartan kilt with bullet holes and name personalisation [enlargement inset] belonging to Pipe Major Robert Roy and worn at the Battle for the Relief of the Tobruk Garrison, November 1941.
(A1041 – on display)
The gun in the foreground is a STEN Mark 2 submachine gun.

43—Section of Royal Stewart piper's plaid gifted to Lieutenant Colonel Kydd by Pipe Major Robert Roy. (2013.267 – in store)

44—Hair sporran belonging to Regimental Sergeant Major Robert Roy.
(2012.94.3 – in store)

45—Tam O'Shanter worn by Pipe Major Robert Roy. (2012.31 - on display)

ABOUT THE AUTHOR

ALICE SOPER spent most of her career in the UK and Germany in the field of education: as a class teacher, learning support teacher, deputy headteacher, adviser, and latterly as a Registered Inspector of Schools. After returning to Fife she became a local councillor – a role she undertook until 2010. She has four grandchildren.

Along with her husband, Major (retd) Les Soper, Alice is a member of the Friends of The Black Watch Castle & Museum. Both volunteer with several local community groups including: Growing Kirkcaldy, Beveridge Park Development Group, Kirkcaldy Civic Society, Kirkcaldy West Community Council, and Kirkcaldy Ingolstadt Association.

When clearing her late mother's house in 2011, Alice discovered a suitcase full of old papers, newspaper cuttings, photographs, and two silver piping cups which had belonged to her late father, Robert Roy MBE, DCM; and so, began the research into his family history and extremely interesting life.

———

FURTHER READING

SCOUT JOE CASSELLS—*The Black Watch. A Record in Action* (New York: Doubleday, Page & Company, 1918)

ALAN CLARK—*The Fall of Crete* (Anthony Bland Ltd, 1962)

ROY FARRAN—*Winged Dagger: Adventures on Special Service* (Cassell Military Paperbacks, 1948)

BERNARD FERGUSSON—*The Black Watch and the King's Enemies* (Glasgow: Collins, 1950)

BERNARD FERGUSSON—*The Black Watch: a short history* (Glasgow: Collins, 1958)

JOHN GREHAN and MARTIN MACE—*Operations in North Africa and the Middle East 1939-1942: Tobruk, Crete, Syria and East Africa* (Barnsley: Pen & Sword Military, 2015)

STEPHEN LINDSAY and THE BLACK WATCH PHOTOGRAPHIC ARCHIVE—*The Black Watch: The Black Watch Photography Archive* (Stroud: Tempus Publishing, 2000)

ERIC LINKLATER and ANDRO LINKLATER—*Black Watch: History of the Royal Highland Regiment* (London: Barrie & Jenkins, 1977)

ROBERT LYMAN—*The Longest Siege: Tobruk – The Battle That Saved North Africa* (London: Macmillan, 2010)

YANNIS PREKATSOUNAKIS—*The Battle for Heraklion. Crete 1941: The Campaign Revealed Through Allied and Axis Accounts* (Warwick: Helion & Company, 2015)

VICTORIA SCHOFIELD—*The Black Watch: Fighting in the Frontline, 1899-2006* (London: Head of Zeus, 2017)

GORDON THORBURN—*Jocks in the Jungle: The Black Watch and Cameronians as Chindits* (Barnsley: Pen & Sword Military, 2012)

THE PUBLISHER

Tippermuir Books Ltd (*est.* 2009) is an independent publishing company based in Perth, Scotland.

OTHER TITLES FROM TIPPERMUIR BOOKS

Spanish Thermopylae (Paul S. Philippou, 2009)

Battleground Perthshire
(Paul S. Philippou & Robert A. Hands, 2009)

Perth: Street by Street
(Paul S. Philippou and Roben Antoniewicz, 2012)

Born in Perthshire
(Paul S. Philippou and Robert A. Hands, 2012)

In Spain with Orwell (Christopher Hall, 2013)

Trust (Ajay Close, 2014)

Perth: As Others Saw Us (Donald Paton, 2014)

Love All (Dorothy L. Sayers, 2015)

A Chocolate Soldier (David W. Millar, 2016)

The Early Photographers of Perthshire
(Roben Antoniewicz and Paul S. Philippou, 2016)

Taking Detective Novels Seriously:
The Collected Crime Reviews of Dorothy L. Sayers
(Dorothy L. Sayers and Martin Edwards, 2017)

Walking with Ghosts (Alan J. Laing, 2017)

No Fair City: Dark Tales From Perth's Past
(Gary Knight, 2017)

The Tale o the Wee Mowdie that
wantit tae ken wha keeched on his heid
(Werner Holzwarth and Wolf Erlbruch,
translated by Matthew Mackie, 2017)

Hunters: Wee Stories from the Crescent:
A Reminiscence of Perth's Hunter Crescent
(Anthony Camilleri, 2017)

Flipstones (Jim Mackintosh, 2018)

Perth & Kinross: A Pocket Miscellany: A Companion
for Visitors and Residents (Trish Colton, 2019)

FORTHCOMING

Perth and the Jacobite Rising of 1715-16 (Kathleen Lyle, 2019)

The Scots Emoji Dictionary (Michael Dempster, 2019)

Dr Irvine and the Irvine Memorial Hospital (Rita Isles, 2019)

William Soutar: Collected Poetry
(Kirsteen McCue and Paul S. Philippou (eds.), 2020)

God, Hitler, and Lord Peter Wimsey: Selected Essays,
Speeches and Articles by Dorothy L. Sayers
(Dorothy L. Sayers and Suzanne Bray (ed.), 2019)

BY LULLABY PRESS
(AN IMPRINT OF TIPPERMUIR BOOKS)

A Little Book of Carol's (Carol Page, 2018)

All titles are available from bookshops and online booksellers.

They can also be purchased directly at
www.tippermuirbooks.co.uk

Tippermuir Books Ltd can be contacted at
mail@tippermuirbooks.co.uk